Nestlé®

CLASSIC RECIPES™

Publications International, Ltd.

Favorite Brand Name Recipes at www.fbnr.com

Microwave Cooking: Microwave ovens vary in wattage. Use the cooking times as guide-
lines and check for doneness before adding more time.

Table of Contents

Favorite Cookies

Who can resist America's most popular snack, fresh-baked cookies? Enjoy a warm-from-the-oven batch today!

Original Nestlé® Toll House® Chocolate Chip Cookies

2¼ cups all-purpose flour

1 teaspoon baking soda

1 teaspoon salt

1 cup (2 sticks) butter or margarine, softened

¾ cup granulated sugar

¾ cup packed brown sugar

1 teaspoon vanilla extract

2 large eggs

2 cups (12-ounce package) NESTLÉ® TOLL HOUSE® Semi-Sweet Chocolate Morsels

1 cup chopped nuts

PREHEAT oven to 375°F.

COMBINE flour, baking soda and salt in small bowl. Beat butter, granulated sugar, brown sugar and vanilla extract in large mixer bowl until creamy. Add eggs, one at a time, beating well after each addition. Gradually beat in flour mixture. Stir in morsels and nuts. Drop by rounded tablespoon onto ungreased baking sheets.

BAKE for 9 to 11 minutes or until golden brown. Cool on baking sheets for 2 minutes; remove to wire racks to cool completely.

Makes about 5 dozen cookies

Pan Cookie Variation: GREASE 15×10-inch jelly-roll pan. Prepare dough as above. Spread into prepared pan. Bake for 20 to 25 minutes or until golden brown. Cool in pan on wire rack. Makes 4 dozen bars.

Chocolate Chip Shells

2 cups all-purpose flour

1 1/3 cups (about 8 ounces) NESTLÉ® TOLL HOUSE® Semi-Sweet
Chocolate Morsels, *divided*

4 large eggs

1 cup granulated sugar

1 tablespoon orange liqueur (such as Cointreau) *or* 1 teaspoon
orange extract

1 teaspoon vanilla extract

2 tablespoons (about 1 orange) grated orange peel

1 cup (2 sticks) unsalted butter, melted

Sifted powdered sugar

PREHEAT oven to 350°F. Generously grease and flour madeleine
baking pan(s).

COMBINE flour and *1 cup* morsels in medium bowl. Beat eggs,
granulated sugar, orange liqueur, vanilla extract and orange peel in large
mixer bowl until light in color. Fold flour mixture and butter alternately
into egg mixture, beginning and ending with flour mixture. Spoon heaping
tablespoon of batter into each prepared mold.

BAKE for 10 to 12 minutes or until wooden pick inserted in center
comes out clean. Cool in pan(s) for 1 minute. With tip of knife, release
onto wire racks to cool completely. Wash, grease and flour pan(s). Repeat
with *remaining* batter.

SPRINKLE madeleines very lightly with powdered sugar. Microwave
remaining morsels in *heavy-duty* resealable plastic food storage bag on
HIGH (100%) power for 30 seconds; knead bag to mix. Microwave at

additional 10-second intervals, kneading until smooth. Cut a small hole in corner of bag; squeeze to drizzle over madeleines. Allow chocolate to cool and set before serving.   *Makes about 2¹/₂ dozen madeleines*

Chocolate Chip Shells

Macadamia Nut White Chip Pumpkin Cookies

2 cups all-purpose flour

2 teaspoons ground cinnamon

1 teaspoon ground cloves

1 teaspoon baking soda

1 cup (2 sticks) butter or margarine, softened

$^{1}/_{2}$ cup granulated sugar

$^{1}/_{2}$ cup packed brown sugar

1 cup LIBBY'S® 100% Pure Pumpkin

1 large egg

2 teaspoons vanilla extract

2 cups (12-ounce package) NESTLÉ® TOLL HOUSE®
   Premier White Morsels

$^{2}/_{3}$ cup coarsely chopped macadamia nuts or walnuts, toasted

PREHEAT oven to 350°F.

COMBINE flour, cinnamon, cloves and baking soda in small bowl. Beat butter, granulated sugar and brown sugar in large mixer bowl until creamy. Beat in pumpkin, egg and vanilla extract until blended. Gradually beat in flour mixture. Stir in morsels and nuts. Drop by rounded tablespoon onto greased baking sheets; flatten slightly with back of spoon or greased bottom of glass dipped in granulated sugar.

BAKE for 11 to 14 minutes or until centers are set. Cool on baking sheets for 2 minutes; remove to wire racks to cool completely.

Makes about 4 dozen cookies

Milk Chocolate Oatmeal Cookies

1 $1/4$ cups all-purpose flour

$1/2$ teaspoon baking powder

$1/2$ teaspoon baking soda

$1/2$ teaspoon ground cinnamon

$1/4$ teaspoon salt

$3/4$ cup ($1 1/2$ sticks) butter or margarine, softened

$3/4$ cup packed brown sugar

$1/3$ cup granulated sugar

$1 1/2$ teaspoons vanilla extract

1 large egg

2 tablespoons milk

$1 3/4$ cups (11.5-ounce package) NESTLÉ® TOLL HOUSE®
  Milk Chocolate Morsels

1 cup uncooked quick or old-fashioned oats

$1/2$ cup raisins (optional)

PREHEAT oven to 375°F.

COMBINE flour, baking powder, baking soda, cinnamon and salt in small bowl. Beat butter, brown sugar, granulated sugar and vanilla extract in large mixer bowl until creamy. Beat in egg. Gradually beat in flour mixture and milk. Stir in morsels, oats and raisins. Drop by rounded tablespoon onto ungreased baking sheets.

BAKE for 10 to 14 minutes or until edges are crisp but centers are still soft. Cool on baking sheets for 2 minutes; remove to wire racks to cool completely. *Makes about 3 dozen cookies*

Island Cookies

1²/₃ cups all-purpose flour

³/₄ teaspoon baking powder

¹/₂ teaspoon baking soda

¹/₂ teaspoon salt

³/₄ cup (1¹/₂ sticks) butter, softened

³/₄ cup packed brown sugar

¹/₃ cup granulated sugar

1 teaspoon vanilla extract

1 large egg

1³/₄ cups (11.5-ounce package) NESTLÉ® TOLL HOUSE®
      Milk Chocolate Morsels

1 cup flaked coconut, toasted, if desired

1 cup chopped walnuts

PREHEAT oven to 375°F.

COMBINE flour, baking powder, baking soda and salt in small bowl.
Beat butter, brown sugar, granulated sugar and vanilla extract in large
mixer bowl until creamy. Beat in egg. Gradually beat in flour mixture.
Stir in morsels, coconut and nuts. Drop by slightly rounded tablespoon
onto ungreased baking sheets.

BAKE for 8 to 11 minutes or until edges are lightly browned. Cool on
baking sheets for 2 minutes; remove to wire racks to cool completely.

Makes about 3 dozen cookies

Note: NESTLÉ® TOLL HOUSE® Semi-Sweet Chocolate Morsels,
Semi-Sweet Chocolate Mini Morsels, Premier White Morsels or
Butterscotch Flavored Morsels may be substituted for the Milk Chocolate
Morsels.

Island Cookies

Chocolate-Cherry Thumbprints

2 cups (12-ounce package) NESTLÉ® TOLL HOUSE®
Semi-Sweet Chocolate Morsels, *divided*

1³/4 cups quick or old-fashioned oats

1¹/2 cups all-purpose flour

¹/4 cup NESTLÉ® TOLL HOUSE® Baking Cocoa

1 teaspoon baking powder

¹/4 teaspoon salt (optional)

³/4 cup granulated sugar

²/3 cup butter or margarine, softened

2 large eggs

1 teaspoon vanilla extract

2 cups (two 10-ounce jars) maraschino cherries, drained
and patted dry

MICROWAVE *1 cup* morsels in small, microwave-safe bowl on HIGH
(100%) power for 1 minute; stir. Microwave at additional 10- to
20-second intervals, stirring until smooth. Combine oats, flour, cocoa,
baking powder and salt in medium bowl.

BEAT sugar, butter, eggs and vanilla extract in large mixer bowl until
smooth. Beat in melted chocolate. Stir in oat mixture. Cover; refrigerate
dough for 1 hour.

PREHEAT oven to 350°F.

SHAPE dough into 1-inch balls. Place 2 inches apart on ungreased
baking sheet. Press thumb into tops to make deep depression. Place
maraschino cherry into each depression.

BAKE for 10 to 12 minutes or until set. Cool on baking sheets for
2 minutes; remove to wire racks to cool completely. Melt *remaining*
morsels; drizzle over cookies.   *Makes about 4 dozen cookies*

Chunky Chocolate Chip Peanut Butter Cookies

1 $1/4$ cups all-purpose flour

$1/2$ teaspoon baking soda

$1/2$ teaspoon ground cinnamon

$1/2$ teaspoon salt

$3/4$ cup ($1 1/2$ sticks) butter or margarine, softened

$1/2$ cup granulated sugar

$1/2$ cup packed brown sugar

$1/2$ cup creamy peanut butter

1 large egg

1 teaspoon vanilla extract

2 cups (12-ounce package) NESTLÉ® TOLL HOUSE®
    Semi-Sweet Chocolate Morsels

$1/2$ cup coarsely chopped peanuts

PREHEAT oven to 375°F.

COMBINE flour, baking soda, cinnamon and salt in small bowl. Beat butter, granulated sugar, brown sugar, and peanut butter in large mixer bowl until creamy. Beat in egg and vanilla extract. Gradually beat in flour mixture. Stir in morsels and peanuts.

DROP dough by rounded tablespoon onto ungreased baking sheets. Press down slightly to flatten into 2-inch circles.

BAKE for 7 to 10 minutes or until edges are set but centers are still soft. Cool on baking sheets for 4 minutes; remove to wire racks to cool completely.   *Makes about 3 dozen cookies*

Milk Chocolate Florentine Cookies

$^2/_3$ cup butter

2 cups quick oats

1 cup granulated sugar

$^2/_3$ cup all-purpose flour

$^1/_4$ cup light or dark corn syrup

$^1/_4$ cup milk

1 teaspoon vanilla extract

$^1/_4$ teaspoon salt

1 $^3/_4$ cups (11.5-ounce package) NESTLÉ® TOLL HOUSE®
    Milk Chocolate Morsels

PREHEAT oven to 375°F. Line baking sheets with foil.

MELT butter in medium saucepan; remove from heat. Stir in oats, sugar, flour, corn syrup, milk, vanilla extract and salt; mix well. Drop by level teaspoon, about 3 inches apart, onto prepared baking sheets. Spread thinly with rubber spatula.

BAKE for 6 to 8 minutes or until golden brown. Cool completely on baking sheets on wire racks. Peel foil from cookies.

MICROWAVE morsels in medium, microwave-safe bowl on MEDIUM-HIGH (70%) power for 1 minute; stir. Microwave at additional 10- to 20-second intervals, stirring until smooth. Spread thin layer of melted chocolate onto flat side of half the cookies. Top with remaining cookies.

Makes about 3½ dozen sandwich cookies

Milk Chocolate Florentine Cookies

Mini Chip Snowball Cookies

1$\frac{1}{2}$ cups (3 sticks) butter or margarine, softened

$\frac{3}{4}$ cup powdered sugar

1 tablespoon vanilla extract

$\frac{1}{2}$ teaspoon salt

3 cups all-purpose flour

2 cups (12-ounce package) NESTLÉ® TOLL HOUSE®
   Semi-Sweet Chocolate Mini Morsels

$\frac{1}{2}$ cup finely chopped nuts

Powdered sugar

PREHEAT oven to 375°F.

BEAT butter, sugar, vanilla extract and salt in large mixer bowl until creamy. Gradually beat in flour; stir in morsels and nuts. Shape level tablespoons of dough into 1$\frac{1}{4}$-inch balls. Place on ungreased baking sheets.

BAKE for 10 to 12 minutes or until cookies are set and lightly browned. Remove from oven. Sift powdered sugar over hot cookies on baking sheets. Cool on baking sheets for 10 minutes; remove to wire racks to cool completely. Sprinkle with additional powdered sugar, if desired. Store in airtight containers. *Makes about 5 dozen cookies*

Pumpkin Spiced and Iced Cookies

2$\frac{1}{4}$ cups all-purpose flour

1$\frac{1}{2}$ teaspoons pumpkin pie spice

1 teaspoon baking powder

$\frac{1}{2}$ teaspoon baking soda

$\frac{1}{2}$ teaspoon salt

1 cup (2 sticks) butter or margarine, softened

1 cup granulated sugar

1 can (15 ounces) LIBBY'S® 100% Pure Pumpkin

2 large eggs

1 teaspoon vanilla extract

2 cups (12-ounce package) NESTLÉ® TOLL HOUSE®
    Semi-Sweet Chocolate Morsels

1 cup chopped walnuts (optional)

Vanilla Glaze (recipe follows)

PREHEAT oven to 375°F. Grease baking sheets.

COMBINE flour, pumpkin pie spice, baking powder, baking soda and salt in medium bowl. Beat butter and granulated sugar in large mixer bowl until creamy. Beat in pumpkin, eggs and vanilla extract. Gradually beat in flour mixture. Stir in morsels and nuts. Drop by rounded tablespoon onto prepared baking sheets.

BAKE for 15 to 20 minutes or until edges are lightly browned. Cool on baking sheets for 2 minutes; remove to wire rack to cool completely. Spread or drizzle with Vanilla Glaze.   *Makes about 5$\frac{1}{2}$ dozen cookies*

Vanilla Glaze: COMBINE 1 cup powdered sugar, 1 to 1$\frac{1}{2}$ tablespoons milk and $\frac{1}{2}$ teaspoon vanilla extract in small bowl; mix well.

Jumbo 3-Chip Cookies

4 cups all-purpose flour

1 teaspoon baking powder

1 teaspoon baking soda

1 1/2 cups (3 sticks) butter, softened

1 1/4 cups granulated sugar

1 1/4 cups packed brown sugar

2 large eggs

1 tablespoon vanilla extract

1 cup (6 ounces) NESTLÉ® TOLL HOUSE® Milk Chocolate Morsels

1 cup (6 ounces) NESTLÉ® TOLL HOUSE® Semi-Sweet Chocolate Morsels

1/2 cup NESTLÉ® TOLL HOUSE® Premier White Morsels

1 cup chopped nuts

PREHEAT oven to 375°F.

COMBINE flour, baking powder and baking soda in medium bowl. Beat butter, granulated sugar and brown sugar in large mixer bowl until creamy. Beat in eggs and vanilla extract. Gradually beat in flour mixture. Stir in morsels and nuts. Drop dough by level 1/4-cup measure 2 inches apart onto ungreased baking sheets.

BAKE for 12 to 14 minutes or until light golden brown. Cool on baking sheets for 2 minutes; remove to wire racks to cool completely.

Makes about 2 dozen cookies

Jumbo 3-Chip Cookies

Oatmeal Scotchies

1 $\frac{1}{4}$ cups all-purpose flour

1 teaspoon baking soda

$\frac{1}{2}$ teaspoon ground cinnamon

$\frac{1}{2}$ teaspoon salt

1 cup (2 sticks) butter or margarine, softened

$\frac{3}{4}$ cup granulated sugar

$\frac{3}{4}$ cup packed brown sugar

2 large eggs

1 teaspoon vanilla extract *or* grated peel of 1 orange

3 cups quick or old-fashioned oats

1 $\frac{2}{3}$ cups (11-ounce package) NESTLÉ® TOLL HOUSE®
      Butterscotch Flavored Morsels

PREHEAT oven to 375°F.

COMBINE flour, baking soda, cinnamon and salt in small bowl. Beat butter, granulated sugar, brown sugar, eggs and vanilla extract in large mixer bowl. Gradually beat in flour mixture. Stir in oats and morsels. Drop by rounded tablespoon onto ungreased baking sheets.

BAKE for 7 to 8 minutes for chewy cookies or 9 to 10 minutes for crispy cookies. Cool on baking sheets for 2 minutes; remove to wire racks to cool completely.   *Makes about 4 dozen cookies*

Pan Cookie Variation: GREASE 15×10-inch jelly-roll pan. Spread dough into prepared pan. Bake for 18 to 22 minutes or until light brown. Cool completely in pan on wire rack. Makes 4 dozen bars.

Oatmeal Scotchies

Frosted Double Chocolate Cookies

2 cups (12-ounce package) NESTLÉ® TOLL HOUSE®
Semi-Sweet Chocolate Morsels, *divided*

1¼ cups all-purpose flour

¾ teaspoon baking soda

½ teaspoon salt

½ cup (1 stick) butter or margarine, softened

½ cup packed brown sugar

¼ cup granulated sugar

1 teaspoon vanilla extract

1 large egg

½ cup chopped nuts (optional)

Chocolate Frosting (recipe follows)

PREHEAT oven to 375°F.

MICROWAVE *¾ cup* morsels in small, microwave-safe bowl on HIGH (100%) power for 1 minute; stir. Microwave at additional 10- to 20-second intervals, stirring until smooth; cool to room temperature. Combine flour, baking soda and salt in small bowl.

BEAT butter, brown sugar, granulated sugar and vanilla extract in large mixer bowl until creamy. Beat in melted chocolate and egg. Gradually beat in flour mixture. Stir in *¾ cup* morsels and nuts. Drop by rounded tablespoon onto ungreased baking sheets.

BAKE for 8 to 9 minutes or until edges are set but centers are still slightly soft. Cool on baking sheets for 3 minutes; remove to wire racks to cool completely. Thinly frost centers of cookies with Chocolate Frosting.

Makes about 2½ dozen cookies

Chocolate Frosting: MICROWAVE *remaining $^1/_2$ cup* morsels and 2 tablespoons butter or margarine in medium, microwave-safe bowl on HIGH (100%) power for 30 seconds; stir until smooth. Microwave at additional 10- to 20-second intervals, stirring until smooth. Add $1^1/_4$ cups sifted powdered sugar and 2 tablespoons milk; stir until smooth.

Chunky Milk Chocolate Chip Cookies

2 cups all-purpose flour

1 teaspoon baking soda

$^1/_4$ teaspoon salt

$1^1/_4$ cups packed brown sugar

1 cup (2 sticks) butter or margarine, softened

1 teaspoon vanilla extract

1 large egg

$1^3/_4$ cups (11.5-ounce package) NESTLÉ® TOLL HOUSE® Milk Chocolate Morsels

1 cup chopped nuts

1 cup raisins

PREHEAT oven to 375°F.

COMBINE flour, baking soda and salt in small bowl. Beat sugar, butter and vanilla extract in large mixer bowl until creamy. Beat in egg. Gradually beat in flour mixture. Stir in morsels, nuts and raisins. Drop by heaping tablespoon onto ungreased baking sheets; flatten slightly.

BAKE for 9 to 11 minutes or until edges are lightly browned. Cool on baking sheets for 2 minutes; remove to wire racks to cool completely.

Makes about $2^1/_2$ dozen cookies

Best-Ever Brownies & Bars

Try this time-tested collection of rich,
moist brownies and bars—easy,
home-baked treats for every occasion.

Layers of Love Chocolate Brownies

$^3/_4$ cup all-purpose flour

$^3/_4$ cup NESTLÉ® TOLL HOUSE® Baking Cocoa

$^1/_4$ teaspoon salt

$^1/_2$ cup (1 stick) butter, cut in pieces

$^1/_2$ cup granulated sugar

$^1/_2$ cup packed brown sugar

3 large eggs, *divided*

2 teaspoons vanilla extract

1 cup chopped pecans

$^3/_4$ cup NESTLÉ® TOLL HOUSE® Premier White Morsels

$^1/_2$ cup caramel ice cream topping

$^3/_4$ cup NESTLÉ® TOLL HOUSE® Semi-Sweet Chocolate Morsels

PREHEAT oven to 350°F. Grease 8-inch-square baking pan.

COMBINE flour, cocoa and salt in small bowl. Beat butter, granulated sugar and brown sugar in large mixer bowl until creamy. Add *2 eggs,* one at a time, beating well after each addition. Add vanilla extract; mix well. Gradually beat in flour mixture. Reserve *$^3/_4$ cup* batter. Spread *remaining* batter into prepared baking pan. Sprinkle pecans and white morsels over batter. Drizzle caramel topping over top. Beat *remaining* egg and *reserved* batter in same large bowl until light in color. Stir in semi-sweet morsels. Spread evenly over caramel topping.

BAKE for 30 to 35 minutes or until center is set. Cool completely in pan on wire rack. Cut into squares.   *Makes 16 brownies*

Peanutty Gooey Bars

CRUST
  2 cups chocolate graham cracker crumbs
  $^1/_2$ cup (1 stick) butter or margarine, melted
  $^1/_3$ cup granulated sugar

TOPPING
  $1^2/_3$ cups (11-ounce package) NESTLÉ® TOLL HOUSE® Peanut
      Butter & Milk Chocolate Morsels, *divided*
  1 can (14 ounces) NESTLÉ® CARNATION® Sweetened
      Condensed Milk
  1 teaspoon vanilla extract
  1 cup coarsely chopped peanuts

PREHEAT oven to 350°F.

For Crust
COMBINE graham cracker crumbs, butter and sugar in medium bowl; press onto bottom of ungreased 13×9-inch baking pan.

For Topping
MICROWAVE *1 cup* morsels, sweetened condensed milk and vanilla extract in medium, microwave-safe bowl on HIGH (100%) power for 1 minute; stir. Microwave at additional 10- to 20-second intervals, stirring until smooth. Pour evenly over crust. Top with nuts and *remaining* morsels.

BAKE for 20 to 25 minutes or until edges are bubbly. Cool completely in pan on wire rack. Cut into bars.   *Makes 2 dozen bars*

Peanutty Gooey Bars

Butterscotch Cream Cheese Bars

1^2/$_3$ cups (11-ounce package) NESTLÉ® TOLL HOUSE®
   Butterscotch Flavored Morsels

6 tablespoons butter or margarine

2 cups graham cracker crumbs

2 cups chopped walnuts

2 packages (8 ounces *each*) cream cheese, softened

^{1}/$_2$ cup granulated sugar

4 large eggs

^{1}/$_4$ cup all-purpose flour

2 tablespoons lemon juice

PREHEAT oven to 350°F.

MICROWAVE morsels and butter in medium, microwave-safe bowl on MEDIUM-HIGH (70%) power for 1 minute; stir. Microwave at additional 10- to 20-second intervals, stirring until smooth. Stir in crumbs and nuts. Reserve *2 cups* crumb mixture; press *remaining* mixture into ungreased 15×10-inch jelly-roll pan.

BAKE for 12 minutes.

BEAT cream cheese and sugar in large mixer bowl until creamy. Add eggs, one at a time, beating well after each addition. Beat in flour and lemon juice. Pour over crust; sprinkle with *reserved* crumb mixture.

BAKE for 20 to 25 minutes or until set. Cool in pan on wire rack. Cut into bars or diamonds; refrigerate.   *Makes 4 dozen bars*

Deluxe Toll House® Mud Bars

1 cup plus 2 tablespoons all-purpose flour
$^1/_2$ teaspoon baking soda
$^1/_2$ teaspoon salt
$^3/_4$ cup packed brown sugar
$^1/_2$ cup (1 stick) butter, softened
1 teaspoon vanilla extract
1 large egg
2 cups (12-ounce package) NESTLÉ® TOLL HOUSE®
  Semi-Sweet Chocolate Morsels, *divided*
$^1/_2$ cup chopped walnuts

PREHEAT oven to 375°F. Grease 9-inch-square baking pan.

COMBINE flour, baking soda and salt in small bowl. Beat sugar, butter and vanilla extract in large mixer bowl until creamy. Beat in egg; gradually beat in flour mixture. Stir in *1$^1/_4$ cups* morsels and nuts. Spread into prepared baking pan.

BAKE for 20 to 23 minutes. Remove pan to wire rack. Sprinkle with *remaining* morsels. Let stand for 5 minutes or until morsels are shiny; spread evenly. Cool in pan on wire rack. Cut into bars.

Makes 3 dozen bars

Lemon Bars

CRUST

 2 cups all-purpose flour

 $^1/_2$ cup powdered sugar

 1 cup (2 sticks) butter or margarine, softened

FILLING

 1 can (14 ounces) NESTLÉ® CARNATION® Sweetened
  Condensed Milk

 4 large eggs

 $^2/_3$ cup lemon juice

 1 tablespoon all-purpose flour

 1 teaspoon baking powder

 $^1/_4$ teaspoon salt

 4 drops yellow food coloring (optional)

 1 tablespoon grated lemon peel

  Sifted powdered sugar (optional)

PREHEAT oven to 350°F.

For Crust
COMBINE flour and sugar in medium bowl. Cut in butter with pastry blender or two knives until mixture is crumbly. Press lightly onto bottom and halfway up sides of ungreased 13×9-inch baking pan.

BAKE for 20 minutes.

For Filling
BEAT sweetened condensed milk and eggs in large mixer bowl until fluffy. Beat in lemon juice, flour, baking powder, salt and food coloring just until blended. Fold in lemon peel; pour over crust.

BAKE for 20 to 25 minutes or until filling is set and crust is golden brown. Cool in pan on wire rack. Refrigerate for about 2 hours. Cut into bars; sprinkle with powdered sugar. *Makes 4 dozen bars*

Lemon Bars

Chunky Pecan Pie Bars

CRUST

1 1/2 cups all-purpose flour

1/2 cup (1 stick) butter or margarine, softened

1/4 cup packed brown sugar

FILLING

3 large eggs

3/4 cup corn syrup

3/4 cup granulated sugar

2 tablespoons butter or margarine, melted

1 teaspoon vanilla extract

1 3/4 cups (11.5-ounce package) NESTLÉ® TOLL HOUSE®
Semi-Sweet Chocolate Chunks

1 1/2 cups coarsely chopped pecans

PREHEAT oven to 350°F. Grease 13×9-inch baking pan.

For Crust

BEAT flour, butter and brown sugar in small mixer bowl until crumbly. Press into prepared baking pan.

BAKE for 12 to 15 minutes or until lightly browned.

For Filling

BEAT eggs, corn syrup, granulated sugar, butter and vanilla extract in medium bowl with wire whisk. Stir in chunks and nuts. Pour evenly over baked crust.

BAKE for 25 to 30 minutes or until set. Cool completely in pan on wire rack. Cut into bars.   *Makes 2 to 3 dozen bars*

Chunky Pecan Pie Bars

White Chip Island Blondies

1 cup plus 2 tablespoons all-purpose flour

1 teaspoon baking powder

$^{1}/_{4}$ teaspoon salt

$^{3}/_{4}$ cup packed light brown sugar

$^{1}/_{3}$ cup butter or margarine, softened

$^{1}/_{2}$ teaspoon vanilla extract

1 large egg

1 cup (6 ounces) NESTLÉ® TOLL HOUSE®
    Premier White Morsels

$^{1}/_{2}$ cup coarsely chopped macadamia nuts

$^{1}/_{2}$ cup toasted coconut

PREHEAT oven to 350°F. Grease 9-inch-square baking pan.

COMBINE flour, baking powder and salt in medium bowl. Beat sugar, butter and vanilla extract in large mixer bowl until creamy. Beat in egg. Gradually beat in flour mixture. Stir in morsels, nuts and coconut. Press into prepared baking pan.

BAKE for 20 to 25 minutes or until golden brown. Cool completely in pan on wire rack. Cut into bars. *Makes 16 bars*

Rocky Road Bars

2 cups (12-ounce package) NESTLÉ® TOLL HOUSE®
   Semi-Sweet Chocolate Morsels, *divided*

1 1/2 cups all-purpose flour

1 1/2 teaspoons baking powder

1 cup granulated sugar

6 tablespoons (3/4 stick) butter or margarine, softened

1 1/2 teaspoons vanilla extract

2 large eggs

2 cups miniature marshmallows

1 1/2 cups coarsely chopped walnuts

PREHEAT oven to 375°F. Grease 13×9-inch baking pan.

MICROWAVE *1 cup* morsels in medium, microwave-safe bowl on
HIGH (100%) power for 1 minute; stir. Microwave at additional
10- to 20- second intervals; stir until smooth. Cool to room temperature.
Combine flour and baking powder in small bowl.

BEAT sugar, butter and vanilla extract in large mixer bowl until crumbly.
Beat in eggs. Add melted chocolate; beat until smooth. Gradually beat in
flour mixture. Spread batter into prepared baking pan.

BAKE for 16 to 20 minutes or until wooden pick inserted in center
comes out slightly sticky.

REMOVE from oven; sprinkle immediately with marshmallows,
nuts and *remaining* morsels. Return to oven for 2 minutes or just
until marshmallows begin to melt. Cool in pan on wire rack for
20 to 30 minutes. Cut into bars with wet knife. Serve warm.

Makes 2 1/2 dozen bars

Razz-Ma-Tazz Bars

1/2 cup (1 stick) butter or margarine

2 cups (12-ounce package) NESTLÉ® TOLL HOUSE® Premier White Morsels, *divided*

2 large eggs

1/2 cup granulated sugar

1 cup all-purpose flour

1/2 teaspoon salt

1/2 teaspoon almond extract

1/2 cup seedless raspberry jam

1/4 cup toasted sliced almonds

PREHEAT oven to 325°F. Grease and sugar 9-inch-square baking pan.

MELT butter in medium, microwave-safe bowl on HIGH (100%) power for 1 minute; stir. Add *1 cup* morsels; let stand. Do not stir.

BEAT eggs in large mixer bowl until foamy. Add sugar; beat until light lemon colored, about 5 minutes. Stir in morsel-butter mixture. Add flour, salt and almond extract; mix at low speed until combined. Spread 2/3 of batter into prepared pan.

BAKE for 15 to 17 minutes or until light golden brown around edges. Remove from oven to wire rack.

HEAT jam in small, microwave-safe bowl on HIGH (100%) power for 30 seconds; stir. Spread jam over warm crust. Stir *remaining* morsels into *remaining* batter. Drop spoonfuls of batter over jam. Sprinkle with almonds.

BAKE for 25 to 30 minutes or until edges are browned. Cool completely in pan on wire rack. Cut into bars.   *Makes 16 bars*

Razz-Ma-Tazz Bars

Easy Double Chocolate Chip Brownies

2 cups (12-ounce package) NESTLÉ® TOLL HOUSE®
Semi-Sweet Chocolate Morsels, *divided*

1/2 cup (1 stick) butter or margarine, cut into pieces

3 large eggs

1 1/4 cups all-purpose flour

1 cup granulated sugar

1 teaspoon vanilla extract

1/4 teaspoon baking soda

1/2 cup chopped nuts

PREHEAT oven to 350°F. Grease 13×9-inch baking pan.

MELT *1 cup* morsels and butter in large, *heavy-duty* saucepan over low heat; stir until smooth. Remove from heat. Stir in eggs. Stir in flour, sugar, vanilla extract and baking soda. Stir in *remaining* morsels and nuts. Spread into prepared baking pan.

BAKE for 18 to 22 minutes or until wooden pick inserted in center comes out slightly sticky. Cool completely in pan on wire rack.

Makes 2 dozen brownies

Easy Double Chocolate Chip Brownies

Moist and Minty Brownies

BROWNIES

  1 $^1/_4$ cups all-purpose flour

   $^1/_2$ teaspoon baking soda

   $^1/_4$ teaspoon salt

   $^3/_4$ cup granulated sugar

   $^1/_2$ cup (1 stick) butter or margarine

   2 tablespoons water

  1 $^1/_2$ cups (9 ounces) NESTLÉ® TOLL HOUSE® Semi-Sweet
      Chocolate Morsels, *divided*

   $^1/_2$ teaspoon peppermint extract

   $^1/_2$ teaspoon vanilla extract

   2 large eggs

FROSTING

   1 container (16 ounces) prepared vanilla frosting

   1 tube (4 $^1/_2$ ounces) chocolate decorating icing

For Brownies

PREHEAT oven to 350°F. Grease 9-inch-square baking pan.

COMBINE flour, baking soda and salt in small bowl. Combine sugar, butter and water in medium saucepan. Bring *just to a boil* over medium heat, stirring constantly; remove from heat. (Or, combine sugar, butter and water in medium, microwave-safe bowl. Microwave on HIGH (100%) power for 3 minutes, stirring halfway through cooking time.) Stir until smooth.

ADD *1 cup* morsels, peppermint extract and vanilla extract; stir until smooth. Add eggs, one at a time, stirring well after each addition. Stir in flour mixture and *remaining* morsels. Spread into prepared baking pan.

BAKE for 20 to 30 minutes or until center is set. Cool completely (center will sink) in pan on wire rack.

For Frosting
SPREAD vanilla frosting over brownie. Squeeze chocolate icing in parallel lines over frosting. Drag wooden pick through chocolate icing to feather. Let stand until frosting is set. Cut into bars.

Makes 16 brownies

Outrageous Cookie Bars

$^1/_2$ cup (1 stick) butter or margarine

$1^1/_2$ cups graham cracker crumbs

1 can (14 ounces) NESTLÉ® CARNATION® Sweetened Condensed Milk

2 cups (12-ounce package) NESTLÉ® TOLL HOUSE® Semi-Sweet Chocolate Morsels

1 cup flaked coconut

1 cup chopped walnuts

PREHEAT oven to 350°F.

MELT butter in 13×9-inch baking pan in oven; remove from oven. Sprinkle graham cracker crumbs over butter. Stir well; press onto bottom of pan. Pour sweetened condensed milk evenly over crumbs. Sprinkle with morsels, coconut and nuts; press down firmly.

BAKE for 25 to 30 minutes or until light golden brown. Cool completely in pan on wire rack. Cut into bars. *Makes 2 to 3 dozen bars*

No-Bake Chocolate Peanut Butter Bars

2 cups peanut butter, *divided*
³/₄ cup (1¹/₂ sticks) butter, softened
2 cups powdered sugar, *divided*
3 cups graham cracker crumbs
2 cups (12-ounce package) NESTLÉ® TOLL HOUSE®
    Semi-Sweet Chocolate Mini Morsels, *divided*

GREASE 13×9-inch baking pan.

BEAT *1¹/₄ cups* peanut butter and butter in large mixer bowl until creamy. Gradually beat in *1 cup* powdered sugar. With hands or wooden spoon, work in *remaining* powdered sugar, graham cracker crumbs and ¹/₂ *cup* morsels. Press evenly into prepared pan. Smooth top with spatula.

MELT *remaining* peanut butter and *remaining* morsels in medium, *heavy-duty* saucepan over *lowest possible heat,* stirring constantly, until smooth. Spread over graham cracker crust in pan. Refrigerate for at least 1 hour or until chocolate is firm; cut into bars. Store in refrigerator.

Makes 5 dozen bars

No-Bake Chocolate Peanut Butter Bars

Chocolatey Raspberry Crumb Bars

1 cup (2 sticks) butter or margarine, softened

2 cups all-purpose flour

$^1/_2$ cup packed light brown sugar

$^1/_4$ teaspoon salt

2 cups (12-ounce package) NESTLÉ® TOLL HOUSE® Semi-Sweet Chocolate Morsels, *divided*

1 can (14 ounces) NESTLÉ® CARNATION® Sweetened Condensed Milk

$^1/_2$ cup chopped nuts (optional)

$^1/_3$ cup seedless raspberry jam

PREHEAT oven to 350°F. Grease 13×9-inch baking pan.

BEAT butter in large mixer bowl until creamy. Beat in flour, sugar and salt until crumbly. With floured fingers, press *$1^3/_4$ cups* crumb mixture onto bottom of prepared baking pan; reserve *remaining* mixture.

BAKE for 10 to 12 minutes or until edges are golden brown.

MICROWAVE *1 cup* morsels and sweetened condensed milk in medium microwave-safe bowl on HIGH (100%) power for 1 minute; stir. Microwave at additional 10- to 20-second intervals, stirring until smooth. Spread over hot crust.

STIR nuts into *reserved* crumb mixture; sprinkle over chocolate layer. Drop teaspoonfuls of raspberry jam over crumb mixture. Sprinkle with *remaining* morsels.

BAKE for 25 to 30 minutes or until center is set. Cool in pan on wire rack. Cut into bars. *Makes 3 dozen bars*

Chocolatey Raspberry Crumb Bars

Premier Cheesecake Cranberry Bars

 2 cups all-purpose flour

1 1/2 cups quick or old-fashioned oats

 1/4 cup packed light brown sugar

 1 cup (2 sticks) butter or margarine, softened

 2 cups (12-ounce package) NESTLÉ® TOLL HOUSE®
  Premier White Morsels

 1 package (8 ounces) cream cheese, softened

 1 can (14 ounces) NESTLÉ® CARNATION® Sweetened
  Condensed Milk

 1/4 cup lemon juice

 1 teaspoon vanilla extract

 1 can (16 ounces) whole-berry cranberry sauce

 2 tablespoons cornstarch

PREHEAT oven to 350°F. Grease 13×9-inch baking pan.

COMBINE flour, oats and brown sugar in large bowl. Add butter; mix until crumbly. Stir in morsels. Reserve *2 1/2 cups* morsel mixture for topping. With floured fingers, press *remaining* mixture into prepared pan.

BEAT cream cheese in large mixer bowl until creamy. Add sweetened condensed milk, lemon juice and vanilla extract; mix until smooth. Pour over crust. Combine cranberry sauce and cornstarch in medium bowl. Spoon over cream cheese mixture. Sprinkle *reserved* morsel mixture over cranberry mixture.

BAKE for 35 to 40 minutes or until center is set. Cool completely in pan on wire rack. Cover; refrigerate until serving time (up to 1 day). Cut into bars.   *Makes 2 1/2 dozen bars*

Scotcheroos

Nonstick cooking spray
1 1/2 cups creamy peanut butter
1 cup granulated sugar
1 cup light corn syrup
6 cups toasted rice cereal
1 2/3 cups (11-ounce package) NESTLÉ® TOLL HOUSE®
    Butterscotch Flavored Morsels
1 cup (6 ounces) NESTLÉ® TOLL HOUSE® Semi-Sweet
    Chocolate Morsels

COAT 13×9-inch baking pan with cooking spray.

COMBINE peanut butter, sugar and corn syrup in large saucepan.
Cook over medium-low heat, stirring frequently, until melted. Remove
from heat. Add cereal; stir until thoroughly coated. Press onto bottom
of prepared baking pan.

MICROWAVE butterscotch morsels and semi-sweet chocolate morsels
in large, microwave-safe bowl on HIGH (100%) power for 1 minute; stir.
Microwave at additional 10- to -20- second intervals, stirring until
smooth. Spread over cereal mixture.

REFRIGERATE for 15 to 20 minutes or until topping is firm. Cut
into bars. *Makes 2 1/2 dozen bars*

Classic Cakes
& Cheesecakes

Celebrate anytime with these fabulous cakes and cheesecakes—luscious desserts that are the perfect ending to any meal!

Rich Chocolate Cake
with Creamy Peanut Butter Milk
Chocolate Frosting

CAKE

- 2 cups all-purpose flour
- 1 3/4 cups granulated sugar
- 2/3 cup NESTLÉ® TOLL HOUSE® Baking Cocoa
- 1 1/2 teaspoons baking powder
- 1 1/2 teaspoons baking soda
- 1/2 teaspoon salt
- 1 cup milk
- 1 cup water
- 1/2 cup vegetable oil
- 2 large eggs
- 2 teaspoons vanilla extract
- 1 2/3 cups (11-ounce package) NESTLÉ® TOLL HOUSE® Peanut Butter & Milk Chocolate Morsels, *divided*

CREAMY PEANUT BUTTER MILK CHOCOLATE FROSTING

- 1 package (8 ounces) cream cheese, softened
- 1 teaspoon vanilla extract
- 1/8 teaspoon salt
- 3 cups powdered sugar

GARNISH

- 1 bar (2 ounces *total*) NESTLÉ® TOLL HOUSE® Semi-Sweet Chocolate Baking Bar, made into curls (see Tip)

continued on page 52

Rich Chocolate Cake with Creamy Peanut Butter Milk Chocolate Frosting, continued

For Cake

PREHEAT oven to 350°F. Grease and flour two 9-inch-round cake pans.

COMBINE flour, granulated sugar, cocoa, baking powder, baking soda and salt in large mixer bowl. Add milk, water, vegetable oil, eggs and vanilla extract; blend until moistened. Beat for 2 minutes (batter will be thin). Pour into prepared pans. Sprinkle *1/3 cup* morsels over each cake layer.

BAKE for 25 to 30 minutes or until wooden pick inserted in center comes out clean. Cool in pans on wire racks for 10 minutes; remove to wire racks to cool completely. Frost with Creamy Peanut Butter Milk Chocolate Frosting between layers and on top and side of cake. Garnish with chocolate curls before serving.

For Creamy Peanut Butter Milk Chocolate Frosting

MICROWAVE *remaining* morsels in small, microwave-safe bowl on MEDIUM-HIGH (70%) power for 1 minute; stir. Microwave at additional 10- to 20-second intervals, stirring until smooth. Beat cream cheese, melted morsels, vanilla extract and salt in small mixer bowl until light and fluffy. Gradually beat in powdered sugar.

Makes 10 to 12 servings

Tip: To make chocolate curls, carefully draw a vegetable peeler across a bar of NESTLÉ® TOLL HOUSE® Semi-Sweet Chocolate. Vary the width of your curls by using different sides of the chocolate bar.

Triple-Chocolate Cupcakes

1 package (18.25 ounces) chocolate cake mix

1 package (4 ounces) chocolate instant pudding and pie filling mix

1 container (8 ounces) sour cream

4 large eggs

$^{1}/_{2}$ cup vegetable oil

$^{1}/_{2}$ cup warm water

2 cups (12-ounce package) NESTLÉ® TOLL HOUSE®
   Semi-Sweet Chocolate Morsels

2 containers (16 ounces *each*) prepared frosting

   Assorted candy sprinkles

PREHEAT oven to 350°F. Grease or paper-line 30 muffin cups.

COMBINE cake mix, pudding mix, sour cream, eggs, vegetable oil and water in large mixer bowl; beat on low speed just until blended. Beat on high speed for 2 minutes. Stir in morsels. Pour into prepared muffin cups, filling $^{2}/_{3}$ full.

BAKE for 25 to 28 minutes or until wooden pick inserted in center comes out clean. Cool in pans for 10 minutes; remove to wire racks to cool completely. Frost; decorate with candy sprinkles.

Makes 30 cupcakes

Pumpkin Cheesecake

CRUST

  1 1/2 cups graham cracker crumbs

   1/3 cup butter or margarine, melted

   1/4 cup granulated sugar

FILLING

   3 packages (8 ounces *each*) cream cheese, softened

   1 cup granulated sugar

  1/4 cup packed light brown sugar

   2 large eggs

   1 can (15 ounces) LIBBY'S® 100% Pure Pumpkin

  2/3 cup (5 fluid-ounce can) NESTLÉ® CARNATION®
     Evaporated Milk

   2 tablespoons cornstarch

 1 1/4 teaspoons ground cinnamon

   1/2 teaspoon ground nutmeg

TOPPING

   1 container (16 ounces) sour cream, at room temperature

  1/3 cup granulated sugar

   1 teaspoon vanilla extract

PREHEAT oven to 350°F.

For Crust

COMBINE graham cracker crumbs, butter and granulated sugar in
medium bowl. Press onto bottom and 1 inch up side of 9-inch springform
pan. Bake for 6 to 8 minutes (do not allow to brown). Cool on wire rack
for 10 minutes.

For Filling

BEAT cream cheese, granulated sugar and brown sugar in large mixer bowl until fluffy. Beat in eggs, pumpkin and evaporated milk. Add cornstarch, cinnamon and nutmeg; beat well. Pour into crust.

BAKE for 55 to 60 minutes or until edge is set but center still moves slightly.

For Topping

MIX sour cream, granulated sugar and vanilla extract in small bowl; mix well. Spread over surface of warm cheesecake. Bake for 5 minutes. Cool on wire rack. Refrigerate for several hours or overnight. Remove side of springform pan.

Makes 16 servings

Pumpkin Cheesecake

Chocolate Intensity

CAKE
>   4 bars (8-ounce box) NESTLÉ® TOLL HOUSE® Unsweetened
>   Chocolate Baking Bars, broken into pieces
> $^1/_2$ cup (1 stick) butter, softened
>   1 $^1/_2$ cups granulated sugar
>   3 large eggs
>   2 teaspoons vanilla extract
> $^2/_3$ cup all-purpose flour
>   Powdered sugar (optional)

COFFEE CRÈME ANGLAISE SAUCE
>   4 large egg yolks, lightly beaten
> $^1/_3$ cup granulated sugar
>   1 tablespoon TASTER'S CHOICE® 100% Pure Instant Coffee
>   1 $^1/_2$ cups milk
>   1 teaspoon vanilla extract

PREHEAT oven to 350°F. Grease 9-inch springform pan.

For Cake

MICROWAVE baking bars in medium, microwave-safe bowl on
HIGH (100%) power for 1 minute; stir. Microwave at additional
10- to 20-second intervals, stirring until smooth; cool to lukewarm.

BEAT butter, granulated sugar, eggs and vanilla extract in small mixer
bowl for about 4 minutes or until thick and pale yellow. Beat in melted
chocolate. Gradually beat in flour. Spread into prepared springform pan.

BAKE for 25 to 28 minutes or until wooden pick inserted in center
comes out moist. Cool in pan on wire rack for 15 minutes. Loosen and

remove side of pan; cool completely. Sprinkle with powdered sugar; serve with Coffee Crème Anglaise Sauce.

For Coffee Crème Anglaise Sauce
PLACE egg yolks in medium bowl. Combine granulated sugar and Taster's Choice in medium saucepan; stir in milk. Cook over medium heat, stirring constantly, until mixture comes just to a very gentle boil. Remove from heat. Gradually whisk *half* of hot milk mixture into egg yolks; return mixture to saucepan. Cook, stirring constantly, for 3 to 4 minutes or until mixture is slightly thickened. Strain into small bowl; stir in vanilla extract. Cover; refrigerate. *Makes 10 to 12 servings*

Chocolate Intensity

Mocha Dream Cake

CAKE

1 1/2 cups hot water

1 tablespoon TASTER'S CHOICE® 100% Pure Instant Coffee

1 cup NESTLÉ® CARNATION® COFFEE-MATE® Powdered Coffee Creamer

2 1/3 cups all-purpose flour, *divided*

1 1/2 teaspoons baking soda

1 1/3 cups (8 ounces) NESTLÉ® TOLL HOUSE® Premier White Morsels

1/3 cup vegetable oil

1 2/3 cups granulated sugar

4 large eggs

2/3 cup (5 fluid-ounce can) NESTLÉ® CARNATION® Evaporated Milk

2 tablespoons white vinegar

1 teaspoon vanilla extract

2/3 cup NESTLÉ® TOLL HOUSE® Baking Cocoa

FROSTING

2/3 cup NESTLÉ® TOLL HOUSE® Premier White Morsels

1/3 cup butter or margarine

1 tablespoon TASTER'S CHOICE® 100% Pure Instant Coffee

1 1/2 teaspoons water

2 packages (3 ounces *each*) cream cheese, softened

4 to 4 1/2 cups powdered sugar

PREHEAT oven to 350°F. Grease and flour two 9-inch-round cake pans.

slightly. Place in refrigerator immediately; refrigerate for 2 hours or until firm. Remove side of springform pan.   *Makes 12 to 14 servings*

Note: Cheesecake may be baked in 13×9-inch pan. Prepare as above. Bake in preheated 300°F. oven for 20 minutes. Cover loosely with aluminum foil. Bake for additional 20 to 30 minutes.

Chocolate Chip Cheesecake

Vermont Spice Cake

CAKE

    3 cups all-purpose flour
 3^1/$_2$ teaspoons baking powder
    2 teaspoons pumpkin pie spice
    1 teaspoon baking soda
   ^{3}/$_4$ teaspoon ground nutmeg
   ^{1}/$_2$ teaspoon salt
 1^1/$_2$ cups granulated sugar
   ^{3}/$_4$ cup (1^1/$_2$ sticks) butter, softened
    3 large eggs
 1^1/$_2$ cups LIBBY'S® 100% Pure Pumpkin
   ^{1}/$_2$ cup NESTLÉ® CARNATION® Evaporated Milk
   ^{1}/$_4$ cup water
 1^1/$_2$ teaspoons vanilla extract

MAPLE FROSTING

   11 ounces cream cheese, softened
   ^{1}/$_3$ cup butter, softened
 3^1/$_2$ cups sifted powdered sugar
    2 to 3 teaspoons maple flavoring
      Orange peel twists, fresh mint, chopped nuts or nut halves
      (optional)

PREHEAT oven to 325°F. Grease and flour two 9-inch-round
cake pans.

For Cake

COMBINE flour, baking powder, pumpkin pie spice, baking soda, nutmeg
and salt in small bowl. Beat granulated sugar and butter in large

continued on page 64

Vermont Spice Cake

Vermont Spice Cake, continued

mixer bowl until creamy. Add eggs; beat for 2 minutes. Beat in pumpkin, evaporated milk, water and vanilla extract. Gradually beat in flour mixture. Spread evenly into prepared cake pans.

BAKE for 35 to 40 minutes or until wooden pick inserted in center comes out clean. Cool in pans on wire racks for 15 minutes; remove to wire racks to cool completely.

For Maple Frosting
BEAT cream cheese, butter and powdered sugar in large mixer bowl until fluffy. Add maple flavoring; mix well.

To Assemble
CUT each layer in half horizontally with long, serrated knife. Frost between layers and on top of cake, leaving side unfrosted. Garnish as desired.   *Makes 12 servings*

Note: To make a 2-layer cake, frost between layers, over top and on side of cake.

Choco-holic Cake

1 package (18.25 ounces) chocolate cake mix

1 package (3.4 ounces) chocolate instant pudding and
   pie filling mix

1 cup milk

$^1/_2$ cup sour cream

4 large eggs

2 cups (12-ounce package) NESTLÉ® TOLL HOUSE®
   Semi-Sweet Chocolate Morsels

1 cup chopped walnuts

Powdered sugar

Raspberries (optional)

PREHEAT oven to 350°F. Grease and flour 12-cup bundt pan or other round tube pan.

COMBINE cake mix, pudding mix, milk, sour cream and eggs in large mixer bowl. Beat on low speed just until blended. Beat on high speed for 2 minutes. Stir in morsels and nuts. Pour into prepared bundt pan or other tube pan.

BAKE for 55 to 65 minutes or until wooden pick inserted in cake comes out clean.

COOL in pan for 20 minutes. Invert onto wire rack to cool completely. Sprinkle with powdered sugar; garnish with raspberries.

Makes 24 servings

Premier White Lemony Cheesecake

CRUST

   6 tablespoons butter or margarine, softened

   1/4 cup granulated sugar

   1 1/4 cups all-purpose flour

   1 large egg yolk

   1/8 teaspoon salt

FILLING

   6 bars (*two* 6-ounce boxes) NESTLÉ® TOLL HOUSE® Premier White Baking Bars, broken into pieces *or* 2 cups (12-ounce package) NESTLÉ® TOLL HOUSE® Premier White Morsels

   1/2 cup heavy whipping cream

   2 packages (8 ounces *each*) cream cheese, softened

   1 tablespoon lemon juice

   2 teaspoons grated lemon peel

   1/4 teaspoon salt

   3 large egg whites

   1 large egg

PREHEAT oven to 350°F. Lightly grease 9-inch springform pan.

For Crust

BEAT butter and sugar in small mixer bowl until creamy. Beat in flour, egg yolk and salt. Press mixture onto bottom and 1 inch up side of prepared pan.

BAKE for 14 to 16 minutes or until crust is set.

For Filling

MICROWAVE baking bars and whipping cream in medium, microwave-safe bowl on MEDIUM-HIGH (70%) power for 1 minute; stir. Microwave at additional 10- to 20-second intervals, stirring until smooth.

BEAT cream cheese, lemon juice, lemon peel and salt in large mixer bowl until smooth. Gradually beat in melted baking bars. Beat in egg whites and egg. Pour into crust.

BAKE for 35 to 40 minutes or until edge is lightly browned. Run knife around edge of cheesecake. Cool completely in pan on wire rack. Refrigerate for several hours or overnight. Remove side of springform pan. Garnish as desired. *Makes 12 to 16 servings*

Premier White Lemony Cheesecake

Pumpkin Cake Roll
with Cream Cheese Filling

CAKE

    Powdered sugar

  3/4 cup all-purpose flour

  1/2 teaspoon baking powder

  1/2 teaspoon baking soda

  1/2 teaspoon ground cinnamon

  1/2 teaspoon ground cloves

  1/4 teaspoon salt

  3 large eggs

  1 cup granulated sugar

  2/3 cup LIBBY'S® 100% Pure Pumpkin

  1 cup chopped walnuts (optional)

FILLING

  1 package (8 ounces) cream cheese, softened

  1 cup sifted powdered sugar

  6 tablespoons butter or margarine, softened

  1 teaspoon vanilla extract

  Powdered sugar (optional)

For Cake

PREHEAT oven to 375°F. Grease 15×10-inch jelly-roll pan; line with wax paper. Grease and flour paper. Sprinkle clean towel with powdered sugar.

COMBINE flour, baking powder, baking soda, cinnamon, cloves and salt in small bowl. Beat eggs and granulated sugar in large mixer bowl until thick. Beat in pumpkin. Stir in flour mixture. Spread evenly into prepared pan. Sprinkle with nuts.

BAKE for 13 to 15 minutes or until top of cake springs back when touched. Immediately loosen and turn cake onto prepared towel. Carefully peel off paper. Roll up cake and towel together, starting with narrow end. Cool on wire rack.

For Filling

BEAT cream cheese, powdered sugar, butter and vanilla extract in small mixer bowl until smooth. Carefully unroll cake; remove towel. Spread cream cheese mixture over cake. Reroll cake. Wrap in plastic wrap and refrigerate at least one hour. Sprinkle with powdered sugar before serving.

Makes 10 servings

Pumpkin Cake Roll with Cream Cheese Filling

Triple Chip Cheesecake

CRUST

   1 3/4 cups chocolate graham cracker crumbs

   1/3 cup butter or margarine, melted

FILLING

   3 packages (8 ounces *each*) cream cheese, softened

   3/4 cup granulated sugar

   1/2 cup sour cream

   3 tablespoons all-purpose flour

   1 1/2 teaspoons vanilla extract

   3 large eggs

   1 cup (6 ounces) NESTLÉ® TOLL HOUSE® Butterscotch
      Flavored Morsels

   1 cup (6 ounces) NESTLÉ® TOLL HOUSE® Semi-Sweet
      Chocolate Morsels

   1 cup (6 ounces) NESTLÉ® TOLL HOUSE® Premier
      White Morsels

TOPPING

   1 tablespoon *each* NESTLÉ® TOLL HOUSE® Butterscotch
      Flavored Morsels, Semi-Sweet Chocolate Morsels and
      Premier White Morsels

PREHEAT oven to 300°F. Grease 9-inch springform pan.

For Crust

COMBINE crumbs and butter in small bowl. Press onto bottom and
1 inch up side of prepared pan.

For Filling

BEAT cream cheese and granulated sugar in large mixer bowl until smooth. Add sour cream, flour and vanilla extract; mix well. Add eggs; beat on low speed until combined. Melt butterscotch morsels according to package directions. Stir until smooth. Add *1 1/2 cups* batter to melted morsels. Pour into crust. Repeat procedure with semi-sweet morsels. Carefully spoon over butterscotch layer. Melt Premier White morsels according to package directions and blend into *remaining* batter in mixer bowl. Carefully pour over semi-sweet layer.

BAKE for 1 hour 10 to 15 minutes or until center is almost set. Cool in pan on wire rack for 10 minutes. Run knife around edge of cheesecake. Let stand for 1 hour.

For Topping

PLACE each flavor of morsels separately into three small, *heavy-duty* resealable plastic food storage bags. Microwave on HIGH (100%) power for 20 seconds; knead bags to mix. Microwave at additional 10-second intervals, kneading until smooth. Cut small hole in corner of each bag; squeeze to drizzle over cheesecake. Refrigerate for at least 3 hours or overnight. Remove side of pan.   *Makes 12 to 16 servings*

71

Irresistible Pies

Pie lovers will adore our famous Nestlé® Toll House® Chocolate Chip Pie and Libby's® Famous Pumpkin Pie. Few can resist these spectacular pies. They're perfect anytime.

Libby's® Famous Pumpkin Pie

$^3/_4$ cup granulated sugar

1 teaspoon ground cinnamon

$^1/_2$ teaspoon salt

$^1/_2$ teaspoon ground ginger

$^1/_4$ teaspoon ground cloves

2 large eggs

1 can (15 ounces) LIBBY'S® 100% Pure Pumpkin

1 can (12 fluid ounces) NESTLÉ® CARNATION®
   Evaporated Milk

1 *unbaked* 9-inch (4-cup volume) deep-dish pie shell
   Whipped cream

MIX sugar, cinnamon, salt, ginger and cloves in small bowl. Beat eggs in large bowl. Stir in pumpkin and sugar-spice mixture. Gradually stir in evaporated milk.

POUR into pie shell.

BAKE in preheated 425°F. oven for 15 minutes. Reduce temperature to 350°F.; bake for 40 to 50 minutes or until knife inserted near center comes out clean. Cool on wire rack for 2 hours. Serve immediately or refrigerate. Top with whipped cream before serving.   *Makes 8 servings*

Note: Do not freeze, as this will cause the crust to separate from the filling.

Tip: 1$^3/_4$ teaspoons pumpkin pie spice may be substituted for cinnamon, ginger and cloves; however, the taste will be slightly different.

Chocolate Truffle Tart

CRUST

   $^2/_3$ cup all-purpose flour

   $^1/_2$ cup powdered sugar

   $^1/_2$ cup ground walnuts

   6 tablespoons butter or margarine, softened

   $^1/_3$ cup NESTLÉ® TOLL HOUSE® Baking Cocoa

FILLING

   1 $^1/_4$ cups heavy whipping cream

   $^1/_4$ cup granulated sugar

   2 cups (12-ounce package) NESTLÉ® TOLL HOUSE®
      Semi-Sweet Chocolate Morsels

   2 tablespoons seedless raspberry jam

   Sweetened whipped cream (optional)

   Fresh raspberries (optional)

For Crust

PREHEAT oven to 350°F.

BEAT flour, powdered sugar, nuts, butter and cocoa in large mixer bowl until soft dough forms. Press dough onto bottom and up side of ungreased 9- or 9$^1/_2$-inch fluted tart pan with removable bottom or 9-inch pie plate.

BAKE for 12 to 14 minutes or until puffed. Cool completely in pan on wire rack.

For Filling

BRING cream and granulated sugar in medium saucepan *just to a boil*, stirring occasionally. Remove from heat. Stir in morsels and jam; let stand for 5 minutes. Whisk until smooth. Transfer to small mixer bowl. Cover; refrigerate for 45 to 60 minutes or until mixture is cooled and slightly thickened.

BEAT for 20 to 30 seconds or just until color lightens slightly. Spoon into crust. Refrigerate until firm. Remove side of pan; garnish with whipped cream and raspberries. *Makes 8 servings*

Chocolate Truffle Tart

Pumpkin Cheesecake Tarts

  $^2/_3$ cup (about 15) crushed gingersnap cookies
  2 tablespoons butter or margarine, melted
  1 package (8 ounces) cream cheese, softened
  1 cup LIBBY'S® 100% Pure Pumpkin
  $^1/_2$ cup granulated sugar
  1 teaspoon pumpkin pie spice
  1 teaspoon vanilla extract
  2 large eggs
  2 tablespoons sour cream (optional)
  2 tablespoons NESTLÉ® TOLL HOUSE® Semi-Sweet
     Chocolate Morsels (optional)

PREHEAT oven to 325°F. Paper-line 12 muffin cups.

COMBINE cookie crumbs and butter in small bowl. Press scant tablespoon onto bottom of each of prepared muffin cups. Bake for 5 minutes.

BEAT cream cheese, pumpkin, sugar, pumpkin pie spice and vanilla extract in small mixer bowl until blended. Add eggs; beat well. Pour into muffin cups, filling $^3/_4$ full.

BAKE for 25 to 30 minutes. Cool in pan on wire rack. Remove tarts from pan; refrigerate. Garnish with sour cream. Place morsels in *heavy-duty* resealable plastic food storage bag. Microwave on HIGH (100%) power for 20 seconds; knead. Microwave at additional 10-second intervals, kneading until smooth. Cut tiny corner from bag; squeeze to drizzle over tarts. *Makes 12 tarts*

Carnation® Key Lime Pie

1 *prepared* 9-inch (6 ounces) graham cracker crumb crust

1 can (14 ounces) NESTLÉ® CARNATION® Sweetened
    Condensed Milk

1/2 cup (about 3 medium limes) fresh lime juice

1 teaspoon grated lime peel

2 cups frozen whipped topping, thawed

    Lime peel twists or lime slices (optional)

BEAT sweetened condensed milk and lime juice in small mixer bowl until combined; stir in lime peel. Pour into crust; spread with whipped topping. Refrigerate for 2 hours or until set. Garnish with lime peel twists.

Makes 8 servings

Carnation® Key Lime Pie

Nestlé® Toll House® Chocolate Chip Pie

1 *unbaked* 9-inch (4-cup volume) deep-dish pie shell*
2 large eggs
$^1/_2$ cup all-purpose flour
$^1/_2$ cup granulated sugar
$^1/_2$ cup packed brown sugar
$^3/_4$ cup (1 $^1/_2$ sticks) butter, softened
1 cup (6 ounces) NESTLÉ® TOLL HOUSE® Semi-Sweet
   Chocolate Morsels
1 cup chopped nuts
   Sweetened whipped cream or ice cream (optional)

If using frozen pie shell, use deep-dish style, thawed completely. Bake on baking sheet; increase baking time slightly.

PREHEAT oven to 325°F.

BEAT eggs in large mixer bowl on high speed until foamy. Beat in flour, granulated sugar and brown sugar. Beat in butter. Stir in morsels and nuts. Spoon into pie shell.

BAKE for 55 to 60 minutes or until knife inserted halfway between outside edge and center comes out clean. Cool on wire rack. Serve warm with whipped cream.   *Makes 8 servings*

Nestlé® Toll House® Chocolate Chip Pie

Strawberry Cheesecake Pie

1 *prepared* 9-inch (6 ounces) graham cracker crumb crust
²/₃ cup (5 fluid-ounce can) NESTLÉ® CARNATION®
    Evaporated Fat Free Milk
1 package (8 ounces) fat-free cream cheese, softened
1 large egg
¹/₂ cup granulated sugar
2 tablespoons all-purpose flour
1 teaspoon grated lemon peel
1¹/₂ to 2 cups halved fresh strawberries
3 tablespoons strawberry jelly, warmed

PREHEAT oven to 325°F.

PLACE evaporated milk, cream cheese, egg, sugar, flour and lemon peel in blender; cover. Blend until smooth. Pour into crust.

BAKE for 35 to 40 minutes or until center is set. Cool completely in pan on wire rack. Arrange strawberries on top of pie; drizzle with jelly. Refrigerate well before serving. *Makes 8 servings*

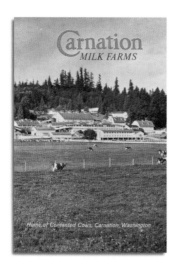

Strawberry Cheesecake Pie

Peanut Butter-Chocolate Brownie Pie

1 *prepared* 9-inch (6 ounces) chocolate crumb crust

$^1/_2$ cup NESTLÉ® TOLL HOUSE® Baking Cocoa

$^1/_2$ cup all-purpose flour

$^1/_4$ teaspoon salt

2 large eggs

$1^1/_4$ teaspoons vanilla extract, *divided*

1 cup granulated sugar

$^1/_2$ cup (1 stick) butter or margarine, melted

$1^2/_3$ cups (11-ounce package) NESTLÉ® TOLL HOUSE®
    Peanut Butter & Milk Chocolate Morsels, *divided*

$^2/_3$ cup heavy whipping cream

Vanilla or chocolate ice cream

PREHEAT oven to 350°F.

COMBINE cocoa, flour and salt in small bowl. Beat eggs and *1 teaspoon* vanilla extract in small mixer bowl; blend in sugar and butter. Add cocoa mixture; blend well. Stir in $^3/_4$ *cup* morsels. Place crust on baking sheet; pour batter into crust.

BAKE for 45 minutes or until set. Cool on wire rack.

COMBINE *remaining* morsels, cream and *remaining* vanilla extract in small, microwave-safe bowl. Microwave on MEDIUM-HIGH (70%) power for $1^1/_2$ minutes; stir. Microwave at additional 10- to 20-second intervals, stirring until smooth. Cut pie into wedges; top with ice cream. Spoon sauce over ice cream.   *Makes 8 servings*

Pumpkin Pecan Pie

PUMPKIN LAYER

    1 *unbaked* 9-inch (4-cup volume) deep-dish pie shell

    1 cup LIBBY'S® 100% Pure Pumpkin

    $^1/_3$ cup granulated sugar

    1 large egg

    1 teaspoon pumpkin pie spice

PECAN LAYER

    $^2/_3$ cup light corn syrup

    $^1/_2$ cup granulated sugar

    2 large eggs

    3 tablespoons butter or margarine, melted

    $^1/_2$ teaspoon vanilla extract

    1 cup pecan halves

PREHEAT oven to 350°F.

For Pumpkin Layer

COMBINE pumpkin, sugar, egg and pumpkin pie spice in medium bowl; stir well. Spread over bottom of pie shell.

For Pecan Layer

COMBINE corn syrup, sugar, eggs, butter and vanilla extract in same bowl; stir in nuts. Spoon over pumpkin layer.

BAKE for 50 minutes or until knife inserted in center comes out clean. Cool on wire rack. *Makes 8 servings*

Easy Coconut Banana Cream Pie

1 *prebaked* 9-inch (4-cup volume) deep-dish pie shell

1 can (14 ounces) NESTLÉ® CARNATION® Sweetened
    Condensed Milk

1 cup cold water

1 package (3.4 ounces) vanilla or banana cream instant pudding
    and pie filling mix

1 cup flaked coconut

1 container (8 ounces) frozen whipped topping, thawed, *divided*

2 medium bananas, sliced, dipped in lemon juice

  Toasted or tinted flaked coconut (optional)

COMBINE sweetened condensed milk and water in large bowl. Add
pudding and coconut; mix well. Fold in *1¹/₂ cups* whipped topping.

ARRANGE single layer of bananas on bottom of pie crust. Pour filling
into crust. Top with *remaining* whipped topping. Refrigerate for 4 hours or
until very set. Top with toasted or tinted coconut.   *Makes 8 servings*

Note: To make 2 pies, divide filling between 2 *prebaked* 9-inch (2-cup
volume *each*) pie crusts. Top with *remaining* whipped topping.

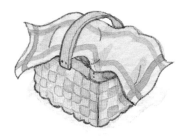

Easy Coconut Banana Cream Pie

Chocolate Mudslide Frozen Pie

1 *prepared* 9-inch (6 ounces) chocolate crumb crust

1 cup (6 ounces) NESTLÉ® TOLL HOUSE® Semi-Sweet
   Chocolate Morsels

1 teaspoon TASTER'S CHOICE® 100% Pure Instant Coffee

1 teaspoon hot water

³/₄ cup sour cream

¹/₂ cup granulated sugar

1 teaspoon vanilla extract

1¹/₂ cups heavy whipping cream

1 cup powdered sugar

¹/₄ cup NESTLÉ® TOLL HOUSE® Baking Cocoa

2 tablespoons NESTLÉ® TOLL HOUSE® Semi-Sweet
   Chocolate Mini Morsels

MELT *1 cup* morsels in small, *heavy-duty* saucepan over *lowest possible* heat. When morsels begin to melt, remove from heat; stir. Return to heat for a few seconds at a time, stirring until smooth. Remove from heat; cool for 10 minutes.

COMBINE Taster's Choice and water in medium bowl. Add sour cream, granulated sugar and vanilla extract; stir until sugar is dissolved. Stir in melted chocolate until smooth. Spread into crust; refrigerate.

BEAT cream, powdered sugar and cocoa in small mixer bowl until stiff peaks form. Spread or pipe over chocolate layer. Sprinkle with mini morsels. Freeze for at least 6 hours or until firm.   *Makes 8 servings*

Chocolate Mudslide Frozen Pie

Pumpkin Dutch Apple Pie

APPLE LAYER

    1 *unbaked* 9-inch (4-cup volume) deep-dish pie shell with high fluted edge

    2 cups (about 2 medium) peeled, cored and thinly sliced green apples

    $1/4$ cup granulated sugar

    2 teaspoons all-purpose flour

    1 teaspoon lemon juice

    $1/4$ teaspoon ground cinnamon

PUMPKIN LAYER

    $1 1/2$ cups LIBBY'S® 100% Pure Pumpkin

    1 cup NESTLÉ® CARNATION® Evaporated Milk

    $1/2$ cup granulated sugar

    2 large eggs, lightly beaten

    2 tablespoons butter or margarine, melted

    $3/4$ teaspoon ground cinnamon

    $1/4$ teaspoon salt

    $1/8$ teaspoon ground nutmeg

    Crumb Topping (recipe follows)

PREHEAT oven to 375°F.

For Apple Layer

COMBINE apples with sugar, flour, lemon juice and cinnamon in medium bowl; pour into pie shell.

For Pumpkin Layer

COMBINE pumpkin, evaporated milk, sugar, eggs, butter, cinnamon, salt and nutmeg in medium bowl; pour over apple mixture.

BAKE for 30 minutes. Remove from oven; sprinkle with Crumb Topping. Return to oven; bake for 20 minutes or until custard is set. Cool completely on wire rack.

Makes 8 servings

Crumb Topping: COMBINE ¹/₂ cup all-purpose flour, ¹/₃ cup chopped walnuts and 5 tablespoons granulated sugar in medium bowl. Cut in 3 tablespoons butter with pastry blender or two knives until mixture resembles coarse crumbs.

No-Bake Chocolate Cheesecake Pie

1 *prepared* 9-inch (6 ounces) chocolate crumb crust
4 bars (8-ounce box) NESTLÉ® TOLL HOUSE® Semi-Sweet
    Chocolate Baking Bars, melted and cooled
2 packages (8 ounces *each*) cream cheese, softened
³/₄ cup packed brown sugar
¹/₄ cup granulated sugar
2 tablespoons milk
1 teaspoon vanilla extract
    Sweetened whipped cream (optional)

BEAT cream cheese, brown sugar, granulated sugar, milk and vanilla extract in small mixer bowl on high speed for 2 minutes. Add melted chocolate; beat on medium speed for 2 minutes.

SPOON into crust; refrigerate for 1¹/₂ hours or until firm. Top with whipped cream.

Makes 10 servings

Extra-Special Treats

Indulge in this special collection of creamy candies and divine desserts— heavenly, showstopping treats sure to please everyone's sweet tooth.

Toll House® Famous Fudge

1 1/2 cups granulated sugar

2/3 cup (5 fluid-ounce can) NESTLÉ® CARNATION®
    Evaporated Milk

2 tablespoons butter or margarine

1/4 teaspoon salt

2 cups miniature marshmallows

1 1/2 cups (9 ounces) NESTLÉ® TOLL HOUSE® Semi-Sweet
    Chocolate Morsels

1/2 cup chopped pecans or walnuts (optional)

1 teaspoon vanilla extract

LINE 8-inch-square baking pan with foil.

COMBINE sugar, evaporated milk, butter and salt in medium, *heavy-duty* saucepan. Bring to a *full rolling boil* over medium heat, stirring constantly. Boil, stirring constantly, for 4 to 5 minutes. Remove from heat.

STIR in marshmallows, morsels, nuts and vanilla extract. Stir vigorously for 1 minute or until marshmallows are melted. Pour into prepared baking pan; refrigerate for 2 hours or until firm. Lift from pan; remove foil. Cut into pieces. *Makes 49 pieces*

For Milk Chocolate Fudge: SUBSTITUTE 1 3/4 cups (11.5-ounce package) NESTLÉ® TOLL HOUSE® Milk Chocolate Morsels for Semi-Sweet Morsels.

For Butterscotch Fudge: SUBSTITUTE 1 2/3 cups (11-ounce package) NESTLÉ® TOLL HOUSE® Butterscotch Flavored Morsels for Semi-Sweet Morsels.

Holiday Peppermint Bark

2 cups (12-ounce package) NESTLÉ® TOLL HOUSE®
Premier White Morsels
24 hard peppermint candies, unwrapped

LINE baking sheet with wax paper.

MICROWAVE morsels in medium, microwave-safe bowl on MEDIUM-
HIGH (70%) power for 1 minute; stir. Microwave at additional 10- to
20-second intervals, stirring until smooth.

PLACE peppermint candies in *heavy-duty* resealable plastic food storage
bag. Crush candies using rolling pin or other heavy object. While holding
strainer over melted morsels, pour crushed candy into strainer. Shake to
release all small candy pieces; reserve larger candy pieces. Stir morsel-
peppermint mixture.

SPREAD mixture to desired thickness on prepared baking sheet.
Sprinkle with reserved candy pieces; press in lightly. Let stand for about
1 hour or until firm. Break into pieces. Store in airtight container at room
temperature.   *Makes about 1 pound candy*

Holiday Peppermint Bark

Quick Tiramisu

1 package (18 ounces) NESTLÉ® TOLL HOUSE® Refrigerated
    Sugar Cookie Bar Dough
1 package (8 ounces) $^1/_3$ less fat cream cheese
$^1/_2$ cup granulated sugar
$^3/_4$ teaspoon TASTER'S CHOICE® 100% Pure Instant Coffee
    dissolved in $^3/_4$ cup cold water, *divided*
1 container (8 ounces) frozen nondairy whipped topping, thawed
1 tablespoon NESTLÉ® TOLL HOUSE® Baking Cocoa

PREHEAT oven to 325°F.

DIVIDE cookie dough into 20 pieces. Shape into $2^1/_2 \times 1$-inch oblong shapes. Place on ungreased baking sheets.

BAKE for 10 to 12 minutes or until light golden brown around edges. Cool on baking sheets for 1 minute; remove to wire racks to cool completely.

BEAT cream cheese and sugar in large mixer bowl until smooth. Beat in $^1/_4$ *cup* Taster's Choice. Fold in whipped topping. Layer 6 cookies in 8-inch-square baking dish. Sprinkle each cookie with *1 teaspoon* Taster's Choice. Spread *one-third* cream cheese mixture over cookies. Repeat layers 2 more times with *12* cookies, *remaining* coffee and *remaining* cream cheese mixture. Cover; refrigerate for 2 to 3 hours. Crumble *remaining* cookies over top. Sift cocoa over cookies. Cut into squares.

Makes 6 to 8 servings

Rich Chocolate Mousse

1 cup (6 ounces) NESTLÉ® TOLL HOUSE® Semi-Sweet
   Chocolate Morsels
3 tablespoons butter, cut into pieces
2 teaspoons TASTER'S CHOICE® 100% Pure Instant Coffee
1 tablespoon hot water
2 teaspoons vanilla extract
$^1/_2$ cup heavy whipping cream

MICROWAVE morsels and butter in medium, microwave-safe bowl on HIGH (100%) power for 1 minute; stir. Microwave at additional 10- to 20-second intervals, stirring until smooth. Dissolve Taster's Choice in hot water; stir into chocolate. Stir in vanilla extract; cool to room temperature.

WHIP cream in small mixer bowl on high speed until stiff peaks form; fold into chocolate mixture. Spoon into tall glasses; refrigerate for 1 hour or until set. Garnish as desired. *Makes 2 servings*

Rich Chocolate Mousse

Chocolate Rhapsody

CAKE LAYER

$^2/_3$ cup all-purpose flour

$^1/_2$ teaspoon baking powder

$^1/_4$ teaspoon salt

6 tablespoons butter or margarine, softened

$^1/_2$ cup granulated sugar

1 large egg

1 teaspoon vanilla extract

$^1/_4$ cup milk

CHOCOLATE LAYER

2 cups (12-ounce package) NESTLÉ® TOLL HOUSE®
Semi-Sweet Chocolate Morsels

$^3/_4$ cup heavy whipping cream

RASPBERRY MOUSSE LAYER

$^1/_3$ cup granulated sugar

2 tablespoons water

1 teaspoon cornstarch

2 cups (8 ounces) slightly sweetened or unsweetened frozen
raspberries, *thawed*

3 bars (6-ounce box) NESTLÉ® TOLL HOUSE®
Premier White Baking Bars, broken into pieces

$1^3/_4$ cups heavy whipping cream, *divided*

1 teaspoon vanilla extract

Sweetened whipped cream (optional)

Fresh raspberries (optional)

For Cake Layer
PREHEAT oven to 350°F. Grease 9-inch springform pan.

COMBINE flour, baking powder and salt in small bowl. Beat butter and sugar in small mixer bowl until creamy. Beat in egg and vanilla extract. Alternately beat in flour mixture and milk. Spread into prepared springform pan.

BAKE for 15 to 20 minutes or until lightly browned. Cool completely in pan on wire rack.

For Chocolate Layer
MICROWAVE morsels and cream in medium, microwave-safe bowl on HIGH (100%) power for 1 minute; stir. Microwave at additional 10- to 20-second intervals, stirring until smooth. Cool completely.

For Raspberry Mousse Layer
COMBINE sugar, water and cornstarch in medium saucepan; stir in raspberries. Bring mixture to a boil. Boil, stirring constantly, for 1 minute. Cool completely.

MICROWAVE baking bars and *1/2 cup* cream in medium, microwave-safe bowl on MEDIUM-HIGH (70%) power for 1 minute; stir. Microwave at additional 10- to 20-second intervals, stirring until smooth. Cool completely. Stir into raspberry mixture.

BEAT *remaining* cream and vanilla extract in large mixer bowl until stiff peaks form. Fold raspberry mixture into whipped cream.

continued on page 98

Chocolate Rhapsody, continued

To Assemble

REMOVE side of springform pan; dust off crumbs from cake. Grease inside of pan; reattach side. Spread *1/2 cup* chocolate mixture over cake layer; freeze for 5 minutes. Spoon raspberry mousse over chocolate; freeze for 10 minutes. Carefully spread *remaining* chocolate mixture over raspberry mousse. Refrigerate for at least 4 hours or until firm. Carefully remove side of springform pan. Garnish with whipped cream and raspberries.

Makes 12 servings

Chocolate Rhapsody

Chocolate Decadence with Sweet Cream

2 cups (12-ounce package) NESTLÉ® TOLL HOUSE®
Semi-Sweet Chocolate Morsels, *divided*

¾ cup butter or margarine, softened

¾ cup granulated sugar

2 large eggs

1 cup all-purpose flour

¼ cup milk

1 cup heavy whipping cream

2 tablespoons powdered sugar

½ teaspoon vanilla extract

PREHEAT oven to 350°F. Line 9-inch-round baking pan with foil. Lightly grease.

MICROWAVE *1 cup* morsels in medium, microwave-safe bowl on HIGH (100%) power for 1 minute; stir. Microwave at additional 10- to 20-second intervals, stirring until smooth. Cool to room temperature.

BEAT butter and granulated sugar in large mixer bowl until creamy. Add eggs; beat on high speed for 2 to 3 minutes. Beat in melted chocolate. Gradually beat in flour alternately with milk. Stir in *remaining 1 cup* morsels. Spoon into prepared baking pan.

BAKE for 40 to 45 minutes until wooden pick inserted in center comes out slightly sticky. Cool completely in pan on wire rack.

BEAT whipping cream, powdered sugar and vanilla extract in small mixer bowl until soft peaks form.

LIFT cake from pan; remove foil. Top with sweetened cream.

Makes 10 servings

Mom's Special Occasion Ice-Cream Cookie Dessert

COOKIES
   1 package (18 ounces) NESTLÉ® TOLL HOUSE®
      Refrigerated Chocolate Chip Cookie Bar Dough

WALNUT MIX
   1 cup chopped walnuts
   1 1/2 tablespoons butter or margarine, melted
   1 tablespoon packed brown sugar

CHOCOLATE SAUCE
   1 can (12 fluid ounces) NESTLÉ® CARNATION®
      Evaporated Milk
   1 cup (6 ounces) NESTLÉ® TOLL HOUSE® Semi-Sweet
      Chocolate Morsels
   1 cup powdered sugar
   1 bar (2 ounces *total*) NESTLÉ® TOLL HOUSE®
      Unsweetened Chocolate Baking Bars, broken into pieces
   2 tablespoons butter or margarine
   1 tablespoon vanilla extract

   Half gallon vanilla ice cream, softened

For Cookies
BAKE cookies according to package directions; remove to wire racks
to cool completely. Chop cooled cookies into small pieces.

For Walnut Mix
PREHEAT oven to 375°F. Grease 8-inch-square baking pan.

COMBINE walnuts, butter and brown sugar in small bowl. Pour into prepared pan. Bake for 8 to 10 minutes; stir well. Cool completely in pan on wire rack.

For Chocolate Sauce
COMBINE evaporated milk, morsels, powdered sugar, baking bar and butter in medium, *heavy-duty* saucepan. Cook over medium-low heat, stirring occasionally, until chocolate is melted. Reduce heat to low; continue cooking, stirring occasionally, for 5 to 7 minutes or until thickened. Remove from heat. Stir in vanilla extract. Cool completely.

To Assemble
WRAP *outside* of 9- or 10-inch springform pan with foil. Spread $1/3$ of chopped cookies on bottom of pan. Top with *half* of ice cream and *half* of chocolate sauce. Combine *remaining* chopped cookies and walnut mixture in medium bowl. Spread *half* of cookie-walnut mixture over chocolate sauce. Top with *remaining* ice cream, chocolate sauce (reserving 2 tablespoons) and cookie-walnut mixture.

PLACE *remaining 2 tablespoons* chocolate sauce in small, *heavy-duty* resealable plastic food storage bag. Cut a hole in corner of bag; squeeze to drizzle chocolate sauce over top of dessert. Freeze for at least 4 hours or overnight.

TO SERVE: Let stand at room temperature for 20 minutes. Remove side of springform pan. Cut into slices.   *Makes 16 servings*

Fruit-Filled Chocolate Chip Meringue Nests

MERINGUES

    4 large egg whites

    $^1/_2$ teaspoon salt

    $^1/_2$ teaspoon cream of tartar

    1 cup granulated sugar

    2 cups (12-ounce package) NESTLÉ® TOLL HOUSE®
        Semi-Sweet Chocolate Morsels

CHOCOLATE SAUCE

    $^2/_3$ cup (5 fluid-ounce can) NESTLÉ® CARNATION®
        Evaporated Milk

    1 cup (6 ounces) NESTLÉ® TOLL HOUSE® Semi-Sweet
        Chocolate Morsels

    1 tablespoon granulated sugar

    1 teaspoon vanilla extract

        Pinch salt

    3 cups fresh fruit or berries (whole blackberries, blueberries
        or raspberries, sliced kiwi, peaches or strawberries)

For Meringues

PREHEAT oven to 300°F. Lightly grease baking sheets.

BEAT egg whites, salt and cream of tartar in large mixer bowl until soft peaks form. Gradually add sugar; beat until sugar is dissolved. Gently fold in morsels. Spread meringue into ten 3-inch nests with deep wells about 2 inches apart on prepared baking sheets.

BAKE for 35 to 45 minutes or until meringues are dry and crisp. Cool on baking sheets for 5 minutes; remove to wire racks to cool completely.

For Chocolate Sauce
HEAT evaporated milk to a boil in small, *heavy-duty* saucepan. Stir in morsels. Cook, stirring constantly, until mixture is slightly thickened and smooth. Remove from heat; stir in sugar, vanilla extract and salt.

FILL meringues with fruit and drizzle with Chocolate Sauce; serve immediately.   *Makes 10 servings*

Fruit-Filled Chocolate Chip Meringue Nests

Dipped Fruit

2 cups (12-ounce package) NESTLÉ® TOLL HOUSE®
  Semi-Sweet Chocolate Morsels or NESTLÉ® TOLL
  HOUSE® Premier White Morsels
2 tablespoons vegetable shortening
24 bite-size pieces fresh fruit (strawberries, orange, kiwi, banana
  or melon), rinsed and patted dry

LINE baking sheet with wax paper.

MICROWAVE morsels and shortening in medium, microwave-safe
bowl on MEDIUM-HIGH (70%) power for 1 minute; stir. Microwave
at additional 10- to 20-second intervals, stirring until smooth.

DIP fruit into melted morsels; shake off excess. Place on prepared baking
sheet; refrigerate until set.   *Makes about 2 dozen pieces*

For a fancy drizzle: MICROWAVE ½ cup NESTLÉ® TOLL HOUSE®
Semi-Sweet Chocolate or Premier White Morsels or Baking Bars, broken
in pieces, in small, *heavy-duty* resealable plastic food storage bag on
MEDIUM-HIGH (70%) power for 1 minute; knead. Microwave at
additional 10- to 20-second intervals, kneading until smooth. Cut tiny
corner from bag; squeeze to drizzle over fruit. Refrigerate until set.

Rocky Road Clusters

2 cups (12-ounce package) NESTLÉ® TOLL HOUSE®
    Semi-Sweet Chocolate Morsels

1 can (14 ounces) NESTLÉ® CARNATION® Sweetened
    Condensed Milk

2¹/₂ cups miniature marshmallows

1 cup coarsely chopped nuts

1 teaspoon vanilla extract

LINE baking sheets with waxed paper.

COMBINE morsels and sweetened condensed milk in large, microwave-safe bowl. Microwave on HIGH (100%) power for 1 minute; stir. Microwave at additional 10- to 20-second intervals, stirring until smooth. Stir in marshmallows, nuts and vanilla extract.

DROP by heaping tablespoon in mounds onto prepared baking sheets. Refrigerate until firm.   *Makes about 2 dozen candies*

Chocolate Mint Truffles

1 ³/₄ cups (11.5-ounce package) NESTLÉ® TOLL HOUSE®
Milk Chocolate Morsels

1 cup (6 ounces) NESTLÉ® TOLL HOUSE® Semi-Sweet
Chocolate Morsels

³/₄ cup heavy whipping cream

1 tablespoon peppermint extract

1 ¹/₂ cups finely chopped walnuts, toasted, or NESTLÉ®
TOLL HOUSE® Baking Cocoa

LINE baking sheet with wax paper.

PLACE milk chocolate and semi-sweet morsels in large mixer bowl. Heat cream to a gentle boil in small saucepan; pour over morsels. Let stand for 1 minute; stir until smooth. Stir in peppermint extract. Cover with plastic wrap; refrigerate for 35 to 45 minutes or until slightly thickened. Stir just until color lightens slightly. (*Do not* overmix or truffles will be grainy.)

DROP by rounded teaspoon onto prepared baking sheet; refrigerate for 10 to 15 minutes. Shape into balls; roll in walnuts or cocoa. Store in airtight container in refrigerator.   *Makes about 48 truffles*

Variation: After rolling chocolate mixture into balls, freeze for 30 to 40 minutes. Microwave 1 ³/₄ cups (11.5-ounce package) NESTLÉ® TOLL HOUSE® Milk Chocolate Morsels and 3 tablespoons vegetable shortening in medium, microwave-safe bowl on MEDIUM-HIGH (70%) power for 1 minute; stir. Microwave at additional 10- to 20-second intervals, stirring until smooth. Dip truffles into chocolate mixture; shake off excess. Place on foil-lined baking sheets. Refrigerate for 15 to 20 minutes or until set. Store in airtight container in refrigerator.

Chocolate Mint Truffles

Chocolate Hazelnut Terrine with Raspberry Sauce

DARK CHOCOLATE LAYER

  2 cups (12-ounce package) NESTLÉ® TOLL HOUSE®
    Semi-Sweet Chocolate Morsels

  $^1/_3$ cup butter, cut into pieces

  $^1/_4$ cup hazelnut liqueur

  1$^1/_2$ cups heavy whipping cream

MILK CHOCOLATE LAYER

  1$^3/_4$ cups (11.5-ounce package) NESTLÉ® TOLL HOUSE®
    Milk Chocolate Morsels

  $^1/_3$ cup butter, cut into pieces

RASPBERRY SAUCE

  1 package (10 ounces) frozen raspberries in syrup, thawed,
    puréed and strained

  $^1/_2$ cup water

  1 tablespoon cornstarch

  1 teaspoon granulated sugar

LINE 9×5-inch loaf pan with plastic wrap.

For Dark Chocolate Layer
MICROWAVE semi-sweet morsels and $^1/_3$ cup butter in medium, microwave-safe bowl on HIGH (100%) power for 1 minute; stir. Microwave at additional 10- to 20-second intervals, stirring until smooth. Stir in liqueur; cool to room temperature.

WHIP cream in small mixer bowl until stiff peaks form. Fold *2 cups* whipped cream into chocolate mixture. Spoon into prepared loaf pan. Refrigerate *remaining* whipped cream.

For Milk Chocolate Layer
MICROWAVE milk chocolate morsels and $^1/_3$ cup butter in medium, microwave-safe bowl on MEDIUM-HIGH (70%) power for 1 minute; stir. Microwave at additional 10- to 20-second intervals, stirring until smooth. Cool to room temperature. Stir *remaining* whipped cream into chocolate mixture. Spread over dark chocolate layer. Cover; refrigerate for at least 2 hours or until firm.

For Raspberry Sauce
COOK raspberry purée, water, cornstarch and sugar over medium heat, stirring constantly, until mixture comes to a boil; boil for 1 minute. Cover; refrigerate.

TO SERVE: Invert terrine onto serving platter; remove plastic wrap. Cut into $^1/_2$-inch-thick slices; serve in pool of Raspberry Sauce.

Makes 16 servings

Best-Loved Breads

Make breakfast and brunch extra special
with these mouthwatering temptations.
From family favorites to new creations,
Nestlé® bakes the very best!

Toll House® Mini Morsel Pancakes

2 1/2 cups all-purpose flour
1 cup (6 ounces) NESTLÉ® TOLL HOUSE® Semi-Sweet
    Chocolate Mini Morsels
1 tablespoon baking powder
1/2 teaspoon salt
1 3/4 cups milk
2 large eggs
1/3 cup vegetable oil
1/3 cup packed brown sugar
    Powdered sugar
    Fresh sliced strawberries
    Maple syrup

COMBINE flour, morsels, baking powder and salt in large bowl. Combine milk, eggs, vegetable oil and brown sugar in medium bowl; add to flour mixture. Stir just until moistened (batter may be lumpy).

HEAT griddle or skillet over medium heat; brush lightly with vegetable oil. Pour *1/4 cup* of batter onto hot griddle; cook until bubbles begin to burst. Turn; continue to cook for about 1 minute longer or until golden. Repeat with *remaining* batter.

SPRINKLE with powdered sugar; top with strawberries. Serve with maple syrup.   *Makes about 18 pancakes*

Blueberry White Chip Muffins

    2 cups all-purpose flour
    $^{1}/_{2}$ cup granulated sugar
    $^{1}/_{4}$ cup packed brown sugar
    2$^{1}/_{2}$ teaspoons baking powder
    $^{1}/_{2}$ teaspoon salt
    $^{3}/_{4}$ cup milk
    1 large egg, lightly beaten
    $^{1}/_{4}$ cup butter or margarine, melted
    $^{1}/_{2}$ teaspoon grated lemon peel
    2 cups (12-ounce package) NESTLÉ® TOLL HOUSE®
        Premier White Morsels, *divided*
    1$^{1}/_{2}$ cups fresh or frozen blueberries
        Streusel Topping (recipe follows)

PREHEAT oven to 375°F. Paper-line 18 muffin cups.

COMBINE flour, granulated sugar, brown sugar, baking powder and salt in large bowl. Stir in milk, egg, butter and lemon peel. Stir in *1$^{1}/_{2}$ cups* morsels and blueberries. Spoon into prepared muffin cups, filling almost full. Sprinkle with Streusel Topping.

BAKE for 22 to 25 minutes or until wooden pick inserted in center comes out clean. Cool in pans for 5 minutes; remove to wire racks to cool slightly.

PLACE *remaining* morsels in small, *heavy-duty* resealable plastic food storage bag. Microwave on MEDIUM-HIGH (70%) power for 30 seconds; knead. Microwave at additional 10- to 20-second intervals, kneading until smooth. Cut tiny corner from bag; squeeze to drizzle over muffins. Serve warm.   *Makes 18 muffins*

Streusel Topping: COMBINE $\frac{1}{3}$ cup granulated sugar, $\frac{1}{4}$ cup all-purpose flour and $\frac{1}{4}$ teaspoon ground cinnamon in small bowl. Cut in 3 tablespoons butter or margarine with pastry blender or two knives until mixture resembles coarse crumbs.

Blueberry White Chip Muffins

Donna's Heavenly Orange Chip Scones

4 cups all-purpose flour

1 cup granulated sugar

4 teaspoons baking powder

$1/2$ teaspoon baking soda

$1/2$ teaspoon salt

1 cup (6 ounces) NESTLÉ® TOLL HOUSE® Semi-Sweet
   Chocolate Mini Morsels

1 cup golden raisins

1 tablespoon grated orange peel

1 cup (2 sticks) unsalted butter, cut into pieces and softened

1 cup buttermilk

3 large eggs, *divided*

1 teaspoon orange extract

1 tablespoon milk

   Icing (recipe follows)

PREHEAT oven to 350°F. Lightly grease baking sheets.

COMBINE flour, granulated sugar, baking powder, baking soda and salt in large bowl. Add morsels, raisins and orange peel; mix well. Cut in butter with pastry blender or two knives until mixture resembles coarse crumbs. Combine buttermilk, *2 eggs* and orange extract in small bowl. Pour buttermilk mixture into flour mixture; mix just until a sticky dough is formed. Do not overmix. Drop by $1/4$ cupfuls onto prepared baking sheets. Combine *remaining* egg and milk in small bowl. Brush egg mixture over top of dough.

BAKE for 18 to 22 minutes or until wooden pick inserted in center comes out clean. For best results, bake one baking sheet at a time. Cool on wire racks for 10 minutes. Drizzle scones with Icing. Serve warm.

Makes 2 dozen scones

Icing: COMBINE 2 cups powdered sugar, $^1/_4$ cup orange juice, 1 tablespoon grated orange peel and 1 teaspoon orange extract in medium bowl. Mix until smooth.

Donna's Heavenly Orange Chip Scones

Butterscotch Sticky Buns

3 tablespoons butter or margarine, *divided*

2 packages (8 ounces *each*) refrigerated crescent dinner rolls

1²/₃ cups (11-ounce package) NESTLÉ® TOLL HOUSE®
      Butterscotch Flavored Morsels, *divided*

¹/₂ cup chopped pecans

¹/₄ cup granulated sugar

1¹/₂ teaspoons lemon juice

1¹/₂ teaspoons water

1 teaspoon ground cinnamon

PREHEAT oven to 375°F.

PLACE *1 tablespoon* butter in 13×9-inch baking pan; melt in oven for 2 to 4 minutes or until butter sizzles. Unroll dinner rolls; separate into 16 triangles. Sprinkle triangles with *1¹/₃ cups* morsels. Starting at shortest side, roll up each triangle; arrange in prepared baking pan.

BAKE for 15 to 20 minutes or until lightly browned.

MICROWAVE *remaining* morsels and *remaining* butter in medium, microwave-safe bowl on MEDIUM-HIGH (70%) power for 30 seconds; stir. Microwave at additional 10- to 20-second intervals, stirring until smooth. Stir in nuts, sugar, lemon juice, water and cinnamon. Pour over hot rolls.

BAKE for 5 minutes or until bubbly. Immediately loosen buns from pan. Cool in pan on wire rack for 10 minutes; serve warm.   *Makes 16 buns*

Stuffed French Toast with Fresh Berry Topping

2 cups mixed fresh berries (strawberries, raspberries, blueberries and/or blackberries)

2 tablespoons granulated sugar

$^2/_3$ cup lowfat ricotta cheese

$^1/_4$ cup strawberry preserves

3 large eggs

$^2/_3$ cup NESTLÉ® CARNATION® Evaporated Fat Free Milk

2 tablespoons packed brown sugar

2 teaspoons vanilla extract

12 slices (about $^3/_4$-inch thick) French bread

Vegetable oil, butter or margarine

Powdered sugar (optional)

Maple syrup, heated (optional)

COMBINE berries and granulated sugar in small bowl. Combine ricotta cheese and strawberry preserves in small bowl; mix well. Combine eggs, evaporated milk, brown sugar and vanilla extract in pie plate or shallow bowl; mix well.

SPREAD ricotta-preserve mixture evenly over *6 slices* of bread. Top with *remaining* slices of bread to form sandwiches.

HEAT small amount of vegetable oil in large, nonstick skillet or griddle over medium heat. Dip sandwiches in egg mixture, coating both sides. Cook on each side for about 2 minutes or until golden brown.

SPRINKLE with powdered sugar; top with berries. Serve with maple syrup.   *Makes 6 servings*

Toll House® Crumbcake

TOPPING

> $^1/_3$ cup packed brown sugar
>
> 1 tablespoon all-purpose flour
>
> 2 tablespoons butter or margarine, softened
>
> $^1/_2$ cup chopped nuts
>
> 2 cups (12-ounce package) NESTLÉ® TOLL HOUSE®
> Semi-Sweet Chocolate Mini Morsels, *divided*

CAKE

> 1$^3/_4$ cups all-purpose flour
>
> 1 teaspoon baking powder
>
> 1 teaspoon baking soda
>
> $^1/_4$ teaspoon salt
>
> $^3/_4$ cup granulated sugar
>
> $^1/_2$ cup (1 stick) butter or margarine, softened
>
> 1 teaspoon vanilla extract
>
> 3 large eggs
>
> 1 cup sour cream

PREHEAT oven to 350°F. Grease 13×9-inch baking pan.

For Topping

COMBINE brown sugar, flour and butter in small bowl with pastry blender or two knives until crumbly. Stir in nuts and *$^1/_2$ cup* morsels.

For Cake

COMBINE flour, baking powder, baking soda and salt in small bowl. Beat granulated sugar, butter and vanilla extract in large mixer bowl until creamy. Add eggs, one at a time, beating well after each addition.

Gradually add flour mixture alternately with sour cream. Fold in *remaining* morsels. Spread into prepared baking pan; sprinkle with topping.

BAKE for 25 to 35 minutes or until wooden pick inserted in center comes out clean. Cool in pan on wire rack.   *Makes 12 servings*

Toll House® Crumbcake

Pumpkin Cranberry Bread

    3 cups all-purpose flour
    1 tablespoon plus 2 teaspoons pumpkin pie spice
    2 teaspoons baking soda
 1 1/2 teaspoons salt
    3 cups granulated sugar
    1 can (15 ounces) LIBBY'S® 100% Pure Pumpkin
    4 large eggs
    1 cup vegetable oil
    1/2 cup orange juice or water
    1 cup sweetened dried, fresh or frozen cranberries

PREHEAT oven to 350°F. Grease and flour two 9×5-inch loaf pans.

COMBINE flour, pumpkin pie spice, baking soda and salt in large bowl. Combine sugar, pumpkin, eggs, vegetable oil and orange juice in large mixer bowl; beat until just blended. Add pumpkin mixture to flour mixture; stir just until moistened. Fold in cranberries. Spoon batter into prepared loaf pans.

BAKE for 60 to 65 minutes or until wooden pick inserted in center comes out clean. Cool in pans on wire racks for 10 minutes; remove to wire racks to cool completely.   *Makes 2 loaves*

For Three 8×4-inch Loaf Pans: PREPARE as above. Bake for 55 to 60 minutes.

For Five or Six 5×3-inch Mini-Loaf Pans: PREPARE as above. Bake for 50 to 55 minutes.

Pumpkin Cranberry Bread

Chocolate Brunch Waffles

2$^1/_4$ cups all-purpose flour

$^1/_2$ cup granulated sugar

1 tablespoon baking powder

$^3/_4$ teaspoon salt

1 cup (6 ounces) NESTLÉ® TOLL HOUSE® Semi-Sweet
    Chocolate Morsels

$^3/_4$ cup (1$^1/_2$ sticks) butter or margarine

1$^1/_2$ cups milk

3 large eggs, lightly beaten

1 tablespoon vanilla extract

Toppings (whipped cream, chocolate shavings, sifted
    powdered sugar, fresh fruit, ice cream)

COMBINE flour, sugar, baking powder and salt in large bowl. Microwave morsels and butter in medium, microwave-safe bowl on HIGH (100%) power for 1 minute; stir. Microwave at additional 10- to 20-second intervals, stirring until smooth. Cool to room temperature. Stir in milk, eggs and vanilla extract. Add chocolate mixture to flour mixture; stir (batter will be thick).

COOK in Belgian waffle maker* according to manufacturer's directions. Serve warm with your choice of toppings.

Makes 10 Belgian waffle squares

*Can also be cooked in standard waffle maker (makes about 20 standard-size waffle squares).

VOLUME MEASUREMENTS (dry)

1/8 teaspoon = 0.5 mL
1/4 teaspoon = 1 mL
1/2 teaspoon = 2 mL
3/4 teaspoon = 4 mL
1 teaspoon = 5 mL
1 tablespoon = 15 mL
2 tablespoons = 30 mL
1/4 cup = 60 mL
1/3 cup = 75 mL
1/2 cup = 125 mL
2/3 cup = 150 mL
3/4 cup = 175 mL
1 cup = 250 mL
2 cups = 1 pint = 500 mL
3 cups = 750 mL
4 cups = 1 quart = 1 L

VOLUME MEASUREMENTS (fluid)

1 fluid ounce (2 tablespoons) = 30 mL
4 fluid ounces (1/2 cup) = 125 mL
8 fluid ounces (1 cup) = 250 mL
12 fluid ounces (1 1/2 cups) = 375 mL
16 fluid ounces (2 cups) = 500 mL

WEIGHTS (mass)

1/2 ounce = 15 g
1 ounce = 30 g
3 ounces = 90 g
4 ounces = 120 g
8 ounces = 225 g
10 ounces = 285 g
12 ounces = 360 g
16 ounces = 1 pound = 450 g

DIMENSIONS

1/16 inch = 2 mm
1/8 inch = 3 mm
1/4 inch = 6 mm
1/2 inch = 1.5 cm
3/4 inch = 2 cm
1 inch = 2.5 cm

OVEN TEMPERATURES

250°F = 120°C
275°F = 140°C
300°F = 150°C
325°F = 160°C
350°F = 180°C
375°F = 190°C
400°F = 200°C
425°F = 220°C
450°F = 230°C

BAKING PAN SIZES

Utensil	Size in Inches/Quarts	Metric Volume	Size in Centimeters
Baking or Cake Pan (square or rectangular)	8×8×2	2 L	20×20×5
	9×9×2	2.5 L	23×23×5
	12×8×2	3 L	30×20×5
	13×9×2	3.5 L	33×23×5
Loaf Pan	8×4×3	1.5 L	20×10×7
	9×5×3	2 L	23×13×7
Round Layer Cake Pan	8×1½	1.2 L	20×4
	9×1½	1.5 L	23×4
Pie Plate	8×1¼	750 mL	20×3
	9×1¼	1 L	23×3
Baking Dish or Casserole	1 quart	1 L	—
	1½ quart	1.5 L	—
	2 quart	2 L	—